Viking Myths and Legends

Enthralling Tales, Stories, and History of the Vikings and Norse Mythology

Free limited time bonus

We forget 90% of everything
that we've read in 7 days...

Get the free printable pdf summary of
the book you've read AND much, much
more... shhhh...

Enter Your Most Frequently Used Email to Get Started

**DOWNLOAD FREE PDF
SUMMARY**

© Enthralling History

Stop for a moment. We have a free bonus set up for you. The problem is this: we forget 90% of everything that we read after 7 days. Crazy fact, right? Here's the solution: we've created a printable, 1-page pdf summary for this book that you're reading now. All you have to do to get your free pdf summary is to go to the following website: **https://livetolearn.lpages.co/enthrallinghistory/**

Or, Scan the QR code!

Once you do, it will be intuitive. Enjoy, and thank you!

Table of Contents

Introduction

Viking myths have captivated audiences for centuries. Eagerly awaited blockbusters, video games, books, and comics have made some of these figures common household names and even Halloween costumes.

But is there more to these Viking gods than is often depicted? This book dives into the stories and myths that are well loved and explores some of the legends that may not be as well known. See why Thor dressed as a goddess and why Loki birthed a horse. How did the Vikings believe the world began? And how did they think it ended?

This book goes beyond just the myths and talks about how Christianity impacted the telling of these legendary sagas. Discover how Viking history interweaves with their stories and why myths and legends are so important to learn about today.

There is so much to unpack in this book. We hope you enjoy this ride through fantasy and history!

Chapter One – An Introduction to Viking History

In 793 CE, medieval Christians in Europe were shocked and appalled at an audacious attack on the peaceful monastery on the holy island of Lindisfarne. It was a vicious raid. The church, according to the scholar Alcuin's letters, was "spattered with blood of the priests of God, despoiled of all its ornaments," after which the strangers, regardless of the carnage they had wreaked on one of the most sacred sites of Christendom in Europe, "trampled on the bodies of saints in the temple of God, like dung in the street." Another chronicler, the monk Symeon of Durham Priory, wrote (albeit some two hundred years later) that they "laid everything waste with grievous plundering, trampled the holy places with polluted steps, dug up the altars and seized all the sea."[1]

The Domesday Stone, a 9th-century grave marker at the priory, depicts a line of seven warriors with their weapons held aloft, preparing for attack. The stone is thought to commemorate this event, which would not be an isolated attack. It was the start of what has become known as the Viking Age.

The Lindisfarne Monastery had been established in the previous century by Irish monk and missionary Aidan, the "Apostle of Northumbria." It held the holy relics of Saint Cuthbert, who legendarily

---

[1] *Volume 2 of Symeonis monachi Opera omnia.* Symeon of Durham. Edited by Thomas Arnold. Oxford University Press, 1965.

healed the sick and expelled several demons from northern England. Pilgrims thronged to his shrine, hoping for miracles or enlightenment. As it became an established center of the Christian faith, kings, nobles, and commoners showered it with gifts of lands, treasures, and other valuables, each hoping to buy salvation.

This holy site could not have been a better target for the three or four ships of the Scandinavian raiders determined to snatch enough silver to buy them land, status, and brides back home. At the priory, there was a whole host of gleaming prizes ripe for the picking and all under one roof. These treasures were barely defended by holy men who had no chance of making any sort of stand against such an onslaught.

As it was recorded in the *Anglo-Saxon Chronicle*, the Vikings robbed and slaughtered without any care for religious sentiment. The raiders crammed their ships with treasure and enslaved monks before setting sail for home, most likely Norway. The people left behind in the church were left wringing their hands in anguish. Christian scholars concluded that it could only be the sinfulness of the people of Northumbria that had left God reluctant to protect the monastery and the holy island.

The Lindisfarne attack was not the first Viking raid. They had already ransacked a Northumbrian monastery at Jarrow, and there had been several attacks in southern England. In 788, three longships landed at Portland. Once ashore, the Vikings slew the reeve of Dorchester, who had ill-advisedly approached them to try and find out the purpose of their arrival and had attempted to take them to the royal manor, according to the *Anglo-Saxon Chronicle*.

The early years of the Viking Age continued in the same vein. In 795, Viking raiders made their first attack on Iona Abbey in the Scottish Hebrides and then made three more raids on that same island in the decade that followed. In 806, the Vikings massacred sixty-eight monks in what has become known as Martyr's Bay. Afterward, many of the Iona survivors fled to the Abbey of Kells in Ireland, which almost certainly saved their lives since the Vikings returned in 825 to burn down the abbey. They killed the rest of the monks who remained.

Vikings came from what is now Norway, Sweden, and Denmark. In the early part of the Viking Age, it was primarily Norwegian raiders responsible for the attacks on Britain and Ireland. The Danes and Swedes tended to wreak havoc on mainland Europe.

The people of these countries were not all known as Vikings. The name has come to define a particular section of the Norse communities: medieval Scandinavian seafarers who were accomplished sailors and adventurers, violent pirates and thieves, and ruthless slave traders.

In Norse society, thralls, or enslaved people, were the lowest class. The Vikings' prisoners of war were often enslaved, and some armed raiders set out on specific slaving missions, sailing from coast to coast in northwestern Europe in search of peaceful communities where young men and women could be taken. There were violent abductions, and some victims were restrained (medieval iron shackles have been unearthed at Viking trading posts at Birka in Sweden and Hedeby in Denmark). The undoubtedly traumatized people who had been kidnapped and taken far from their native lands often passed through several hands, having been bought and then sold at slave markets or to the Anglo-Saxon nobility. Few remained in Scandinavia. After the raid on the priory at Lindisfarne, Alcuin tried to raise funds for the release of the monks that the Vikings had taken.

Although Vikings risked their lives on the treacherous northern seas, most Norsemen quietly farmed their land. They grew crops such as barley, oats, rye, and peas and reared pigs, goats, cattle, and horses to provide enough food for their families and sometimes their extended families. However, the soil was poor, and the benefits of fertilizer had not yet been understood by the Norse farmers in the Middle Ages. The tradition was for the oldest son to inherit the farm, so younger sons generally found themselves having to make their own way in the world. The lure of adventure and comradeship, plus the opportunity to acquire enough silver to buy their own land, must have been a tempting and heady proposition for those young men.

It was a hard life for the Norse in Scandinavia during the Middle Ages for those who were not landowners. The cold climate presented its own difficulties with bitter, freezing winters, and there were periodic shortages of herring, which was a main food source for the population. Paradoxically, in some years, there was a surplus of food to take abroad and trade alongside their usual cargoes of furs, iron, timber, and amber, which they exchanged for gold, silver, silks, and spices from southern traders.

As other nations ramped up their overseas trading, there was always the possibility for the Vikings to indulge in a bit of piracy. As the Viking

Age developed, there was even the possibility of settling overseas in Britain, Ireland, mainland Europe, or even in the small colonies the Vikings established in the faraway lands of Iceland, Greenland, and North America.

Scandinavia was an ideal place to set out to sea and explore the lands to the west. Skilled Norse shipbuilders developed techniques of building strong and fast longships by overlapping planks of ash wood over a ribbed frame that was riveted together with iron pins. Longships made for raiding were symmetrical so that the crew could reverse direction without having to turn the craft around. These ships accommodated a crew of twenty-five to thirty people.

Knarr ships, which were used for trading, were much larger (around sixteen meters or fifty-two feet) and deeper and broader (around five meters or sixteen feet) than the traditional longships. They could carry some twenty-four tons of cargo and a crew of sixty. The knarr ships were not just robust and swift; they were also light enough to be carried or dragged on shore. It was in these knarr ships that Vikings navigated the Atlantic Ocean. Only one of these larger ships has ever been found. It was discovered in the Roskilde Fjord in Denmark; it is now carefully preserved in the local museum.

When the Vikings returned to their homes and hung up their axes, they toiled the soil or worked as craftsmen (such as blacksmiths or shipbuilders), traders, or fishermen. Raids were generally conducted during the summer months when the seas tended to be calmer. That way, the Vikings could return to help with the autumn harvests. Eventually, raiding unprotected, wealthy monasteries became so profitable and lucrative that they found they had no real need to do anything else.

Young men and women were considered to have reached maturity by the age of twelve. Boys at that age were working as adults, managing their lands or working as blacksmiths, sailors, or craftsmen. By the age of twenty, most were married and had become parents.

It is worth noting that women married to Viking farmers were generally considered capable of managing the land in their partner's absence. Women were respected. Female physical abuse was condemned as shameful, and women had better rights than in many contemporary European cultures. For instance, they were able to divorce if they had reason and own property. Although most women were responsible for the homesteads, it is likely that a few had roles in trade and as warriors since scales and weapons have been discovered in excavated graves of females.

The pagan Norse religion and beliefs had been practiced since before 500 BCE. It was polytheistic, meaning there were several deities, both male and female. Worshiping was closely associated with the seasons and the cycles of the year. It was usual for worshipers to congregate in the open air or at natural landmarks. The sacred spaces around these sacred groves, streams, mountains, rocks, or trees were marked by stone or branch boundaries. It is widely believed worshipers left offerings and performed rituals in the hope of ensuring fertility, prosperity, and safety as a part of their daily lives. However, in the remains of multifunctional complexes that include mead halls for public festivals, fenced areas containing a *hörgr* (a kind of altar often consisting of a pile of stones) have been discovered. Some prominent sites can be found on the Lofoten Islands in Norway and Funen in Denmark.

The German medieval chronicler Adam of Bremen wrote an account of the pagan rituals that were performed in Gamla Uppsala in Sweden. He described a temple (*hof*) that was gilded inside and contained three statues of Norse gods. Thor, one of the most important gods, was placed in the center. He ruled the skies and held a scepter. It was hoped that Thor would provide mild weather for farmers and sailors. Odin was represented as a warrior. He was the god of war and victory, whereas "Fricco" (or Freyr) was the god of peace and fertility. Each of these gods had his own priest, and according to Adam, a great festival was held at the temple every nine years. People from all over Scandinavia traveled to attend it.

Human sacrifices did occur. More than seventy-two corpses were left hanging in the surrounding trees, and there was a building dedicated to libation rituals (the pouring of liquid or grains as an offering). The remains of the Gamla Uppsala *hof* have been excavated. The longhouse was more than one hundred meters (over three hundred feet) in length and originally dated to between 600 and 800 CE.

This festival was likely what is known as the *blót* in Old Norse, a common feast that was held for nine days every nine years in Scandinavian and Germanic countries. At Swedish pagan *blót* ceremonies, nine males of each animal species would be sacrificed, including humans.

Although there was no apparent faith leader like in most communities, several Nordic runestones refer to people bearing the title *gothi* in early medieval Nordic villages, especially in Iceland, which the Vikings settled in the late 800s CE. It is possible these officials had a religious standing, but it is more likely they were respected senior figures responsible for political issues, law and order, and matters of faith. The sagas refer to seeresses called *völva* and wise male elders called *thul* who are thought to have been involved in the praising of Norse gods through reciting poetry and singing.

Marriages were a cause of great celebration in pagan Scandinavia. Families found brides for their sons. Once the new couple's inheritance and the bride's dowry had been negotiated, the betrothal was sealed with a gift from the young man's parents. The two families were then bound together, and the contract was sealed at the wedding, which was a public ceremony and feast that often lasted several days.

Birthing a baby was a perilous time for medieval mothers and babies. Norse myths, legends, and sagas give a good understanding of the cultural practices of the time. Expectant mothers sang and performed rituals to the maternal goddesses, such as Frigg and Freyja, for the safe delivery of their children and for a favorable moment for their births. As these deities were thought to be present during childbirth, this natural process was accepted as a part of family and society (unlike some other cultures that considered it an offensive and unclean time).

Nine nights after the baby's delivery, the child was taken to the head of the family, who would sit it on his knee and sprinkle water over it–very much like a baptism. It is possible that the wider family was present and would bring gifts.

After this ceremony, the baby was considered a full member of the clan. If it were to be killed by its parents, they would be considered guilty of murder. (Newborns were, on occasion, killed within their first nine days if it was thought they would not survive.)

Vikings had a strong belief in predestined fate. They chose their ancestors or family names for their children, trusting they would develop qualities and talents from their namesakes.

Viking families set great store by their ancestors, believing they had a great influence over them, even from the far-off lands of the dead. They had a deep respect for death and took cremation and burial rites very seriously. The dead were equipped with their possessions and sufficient food and drink for their journey to the afterlife. Poor people would be buried with a single ax or knife, whereas wealthy Norsemen and women were often laid to rest with several possessions and all manner of luxuries, including sacrificed servants, dogs, or horses in oval graves marked with piles of stones. Some eminent warriors were buried in their longships, and wealthy Danish women have been discovered buried in wagons. Swedish Vikings were more likely to be cremated, with their ashes contained in a clay vessel rather than buried beneath a marked mound.

Viking society was very much based on hospitality. Norse families enjoyed great feasts and celebrations together, and it was considered a point of honor to never turn a stranger away. Young women could be betrothed at the age of twelve, with a celebration that lasted days, followed by a wedding feast during which a great deal of ale and mead would be enjoyed. From art and carvings made at the time and stories handed down through the generations, it is evident they enjoyed wrestling, sports, and games. They played music and sang as part of their festivities.

Since the Vikings weren't Christians, they had little regard for the consequences of ransacking the holy and sacred places of the "new" religion, viewing them as nothing more than badly defended buildings that, more often than not, contained treasure. As pagans, they often missed out on lucrative trading arrangements that Christian merchants agreed upon with each other and were, like Muslim traders, discriminated against for their beliefs. Due to the Vikings' well-earned reputation for violence, pillaging, and ransacking that would last for centuries, merchants from outside Scandinavia were, unsurprisingly, often unwilling to enter into trading partnerships with them.

Viking raids were so brutal and had become so feared that, in 865, the people of Kent (in the south of England) offered to hand over their riches on the condition the Vikings didn't go ahead with the pillaging. This was a revelation for the raiders. They quickly introduced a levy for their regular targets that became known as the Danegeld, which was essentially a payment or tribute to the Vikings so that they would leave a certain region alone. This continued throughout the 10th and 11th centuries. In 991, during the reign of King Æthelred II the Unready, his subjects were taxed to raise ten thousand pounds (in weight) of silver to be handed over to the Vikings. And it didn't end there; three years later, the Vikings returned and were paid another sixteen thousand pounds. In

1002, they came back for twenty-four thousand pounds of silver.

This was a massive amount to hand over, and it could not continue. The Anglo-Saxons were taxed to the hilt and simply could not afford to pay more. The country was bankrupt, the poor were starving, and the people were beginning to question their king's leadership. Alarmed, Æthelred the Unready gave the extreme order that all Viking settlers who remained in England were to be slain on November 13th, 1002, Saint Brice's Day. Thousands of Scandinavians were killed, including the sister of Sweyn Forkbeard, King of Denmark, who swore revenge when he learned what had happened.

The Vikings returned in 1006, and Æthelred was forced to hand over another thirty-six thousand pounds of silver. In a desperate attempt to finally rid his country of the Viking menace, he hastily built a fleet of ships to defend his shores. However, the English proved to be poor sailors in comparison to the Norsemen, and the Vikings had little difficulty in dealing with them. In 1013, Sweyn and his son Canute (also known as Cnut) arrived to take the English throne. Æthelred fled to France.

However, it would be a short reign. After five weeks, Sweyn died of apoplexy, and Æthelred made his return. Canute returned to Denmark, where his brother, Harald II, had been crowned king. Still, Canute had not given up on the English throne. He returned to England in 1016 after raising a formidable army. On his arrival, he learned that Æthelred had died, so Canute managed to get himself elected as the dead king's heir.

As the self-styled "King of all England and Denmark and the Norwegians and some of the Swedes" (used in a letter to his subjects on the occasion of his coronation), Canute is remembered in medieval texts as a fierce Viking warrior and a wise and capable king. He helped restore prosperity to England, albeit after murdering many of the English lords and possible claimants to the English throne.

The Viking Age is considered to have ended in 1066. Just as it had started with the raids on Britain, it drew to a close when the raids stopped at the time of the Norman invasion. Earlier that same year, the Norwegian king, Harald Hardrada, who had left his shores hoping to fight for the English crown, was killed on English soil at the Battle of Stamford Bridge.

By then, the majority of Scandinavians had abandoned their pagan beliefs, having been converted to Christianity. The church did not look kindly on raiding. In the Icelandic saga *Hitdælakappa*, King Olaf tells Björn of Norway to give it up: "Though you feel it suits you well, God's law is often violated." In any case, all the usual targets had become fortified and were far better defended than they had been in the late 700s.

The Norse gods and heroes were not completely abandoned, though. Even today, a small number of people in Denmark still follow the old religion in a similar war to the Vikings, out in the open air with offerings. Some of the ceremonies have been passed down through the generations, and in recent years, there has been a resurgence of paganism in Iceland. The stories of the deities that fascinated and enthralled the Vikings have developed into the Norse mythology that continues to delight readers today.

Chapter Two – A Viking Legend: Grettir the Outlaw

In the Middle Ages, the people of Iceland developed a tradition of collating detailed family histories in the form of long sagas written in prose form. One of these, *The Saga of Grettir the Outlaw* or *The Saga of* Grettir the Strong, was written in the 13th century and relates the story of a Viking hero.

The saga is divided into three parts. The first thirteen chapters relate the lives of Grettir's great-grandfather, Önundur, a Viking raider who lost a foot while fighting against Norwegian King Harald Fairhair in the Battle of Hafrsfjord (sometime between 872 and 900). The king was victorious, and his enemies, including Önundur Tree-foot (as he was then known), fled from Norway to Britain and Ireland. After fighting against King Kjarval of Dublin, Önundur returned to Norway before setting sail for Iceland, where he settled for good.

The saga then moves to the son of Önundur Tree-foot, Thorgrim Grey-head, and his son, Ásmundar, the father of Grettir.

Ásmundar and his wife Asdis had a farm at Bjarg, where they raised their two sons, Atli, a quiet and serious boy, and Grettir, who was born around 997 CE. Grettir was a difficult character. Even as a child, he was rebellious and truculent but also remarkably strong. He is described as having red hair, freckles, and wide eyes. Though his mother loved him very much, his father was wise to his son's nature and knew he was trouble. Ásmundar and Asdis also had two daughters: Thordis and

Rannveig.

Grettir was not much use on the family farm. When he was fourteen, he was sent in his father's place to the Althing (an annual Icelandic government assembly). One morning, he and the other delegates awoke to find their horses had been let loose and their food stolen. Grettir quickly rounded on one of his companions, Skeggi, and accused him of the crime.

Skeggi responded by drawing his ax. Grettir killed him in the fight. Realizing the seriousness of his actions, he claimed the man must have been killed by a troll, but the other delegates were not convinced. Grettir eventually confessed.

Despite his parents offering weregild (blood money) as compensation for the loss of Skeggi's life, Grettir was banished for three years. Before he left, his mother gave him her grandfather Jökul's short sword, or *sax*, sometimes known as Jökulsnautr ("Jökul's gift") since it was a family heirloom, after Ásmundar refused to give him his.

So, Grettir sets sail for Norway. He does little to help crew the ship until there is a leak. Using his great strength and skill, he manages to repair it. Soon afterward, they hit a rock and the ship sinks just off the Norwegian coast where a local landowner, Thorfinn, helps the ship's crew and passengers to safety. Most of the travelers head south, but Grettir chooses to stay with Thorfinn and his family.

One night, Grettir sees an ominous fire in the distance. When he asks about it, he is told that it is the ghost of Thorfinn's father, Kárr inn gamli, haunting his burial mound. Grettir decides to investigate and tunnels into the barrow. In the burial chamber, which is full of riches, is a *draugr*—an undead, zombie-like creature. It is the undead Kárr inn gamli. The *draugr* quickly attacks Grettir.

As they grapple in the burial chamber, Grettir manages to draw Jökulsnautr, his mother's sword, and slices the *draugr*'s head from its body. He returns to the farm with the treasure from the barrow to tell Thorfinn he has defeated the ghost of his dead father. Grettir asks for a particular sword he has found amongst the grave goods, but he is told he will have to earn it.

Sometime later, Thorfinn is away when a small ship of strangers arrives. They tell Grettir they have come to settle a grievance against Thorfinn. To the horror of Thorfinn's wife, Grettir brings them to the house and gives them copious amounts of alcohol until they are very drunk. Then, he guides them to a large outbuilding and locks them in there. Thorfinn's wife, realizing what he is doing, gives him weapons and armor. Grettir goes back and kills them all. When Thorfinn returns, he hands him the sword he had asked for and swears an oath of lifelong friendship.

Grettir leaves Thorfinn's farm to spend the winter as a guest of a wealthy landowner called Thorkell. He soon makes an enemy of one of his host's men, Björn, who is from a very reputable family but is, as far as Grettir is concerned, very self-important and boastful. The two men take an instant dislike to one another.

Soon after Grettir's arrival, a savage, giant brown bear starts rampaging through the area, audaciously killing livestock in front of the farmers and terrorizing the people. When this monster kills cattle and men on Thorkell's land, his men set out to find its lair.

Its den is on a cliff overlooking the sea. The den is only accessible by a narrow path that is precariously close to the precipice. Grettir's enemy Björn boasts that he will kill this bear, but as he makes his way along the path, he hears the huge beast growling and snoring as it sleeps in his den. Björn lays in wait outside, covered by his shield. As time passes, he falls asleep.

The bear awakens and ambles out of its cave, ready to attack another farmer's flock or herd when it espies Björn. With its massive paw, the bear swipes at the shield to send it tumbling over the cliff. Björn manages to scramble to his feet and flees, narrowly escaping the beast's attention.

He returns to Thorkell, full of bluster, where it is decided a posse of eight, including Grettir, will go to slay the bear. They negotiate the perilous path and try to attack the bear in its den. This proves quite a challenge. Grettir takes off his fur cloak to engage in the fighting, while Björn urges the men to fight it while he remains behind, well out of immediate danger. Björn then flings Grettir's cloak into the melee.

The men give up on their fight, and as they start to leave, Grettir realizes he cannot find his fur. It seems that the bear has hold of it. Björn accuses Grettir of throwing it in there himself in order to go back and kill the bear by himself and claim the glory.

Of course, Grettir goes straight back into the cave and grapples with the ferocious bear. Using Jökulsnautr, he manages to slice one of the bear's paws off. Then, as it comes at him, Grettir seizes it by its ears and pulls its head back so it can't sink its teeth into him. This was, he said afterward, his greatest feat of strength.

Grettir and the bear fall from the path and down the cliff, with the bear tumbling to the beach below, sustaining serious injuries. Grettir lands on top of it. He draws his sword and plunges it into the beast. He then climbs the cliff to collect his battered and torn cloak and the bear's severed paw before returning to Thorkell's.

The men are feasting by the time he returns, and they laugh at Grettir in his ragged fur until he puts the paw on the table. He tells Björn it is time he should start giving him respect, but Björn makes it clear that he will not. However, Thorkell has had enough and tells them to put aside their grievances while they are under his roof.

The next spring, Grettir goes north with Thorkell's men while Björn sails to England. The two men meet again at Trondheim in the autumn while heading back to enjoy Thorkell's hospitality. Grettir is delighted with the opportunity to sort out their differences once and for all. After attempting to avoid a fight and then being accused of cowardice, Björn has little choice but to fight Grettir. Grettir kills him.

Björn's men rush ahead to tell Thorkell, who is saddened but not particularly surprised. Grettir returns to Thorfinn's farm. After explaining what he has done, his friend sagely realizes he will need his support.

Björn's brother Hjarrandi is Jarl Sveinn's bodyguard, and he complains bitterly to him about what Grettir has done. The jarl summons Grettir. Although Grettir admits he had been provoked, the jarl decides he must pay weregild to Hjarrandi.

This outcome is not what Hjarrandi had hoped for. So, while Grettir is out and about, he sets upon him, determined to avenge his brother. But Grettir is too strong for him and kills him and his men. Jarl Sveinn is furious and brings a charge of manslaughter against Grettir, who promptly leaves for Iceland, his banishment almost at an end.

While Grettir is struggling to settle into his new life, he hears about a farmer whose pastures are haunted by a wight (another zombie-like, undead entity). To rid himself of this horrible creature, he had hired a very large and strong Swedish shepherd named Glam, who managed to kill the wight but had been killed in the process. When the farmer and his men found Glam's body lying in the snow, they found it impossible to move him, so they were forced to build a mound around him in the pasture.

Soon afterward, Glam became a horrible revenant (another dreadful, undead creature). He starts haunting the local community, killing their animals and banging on roofs during the night. After he kills the farmer's daughter, Grettir offers to help, despite being warned against it.

The revenant Glam kills Grettir's horse soon after his arrival. On the third night, Glam lifts the roof from the farmhouse and steps inside. Grettir quickly makes his attack. As they wrestle, they destroy everything in the hall until Grettir uses all of his strength to force Glam out through the doorway, wrecking the whole of the exterior wall.

As Glam falls to the ground, realizing his end is near, he glares at Grettir, his eyes glowing in the night. Glam utters a curse, vowing that Grettir will never grow any stronger and that his great and heroic deeds will only gain him hatred and exclusion. These words have a great impact. Unable to forget Glam's glowing eyes, Grettir becomes terrified of the dark.

Trying to put Glam's curse behind him, Grettir learns that the new king, Olaf II Haraldsson, is putting together a troop of elite Icelandic warriors and adventurers–a perfect fit for him. Grettir sets out in midwinter to present himself at the king's court.

On the way, the conditions quickly deteriorated. Grettir, frozen after fording an icy river, beaks into a house in search of fire. Unfortunately, when the people inside see a huge man covered in ice, they think he is a troll and fight him, throwing firebrands at him. In the confusion, the house is set alight, and all those inside are killed, including two sons of a popular local chieftain named Thorir.

Despite it being an accident, Thorir is bent on revenge. He makes sure Grettir has no chance of impressing the king, and matters are not helped when Grettir loses his temper and kills a man whose brother, in revenge, kills gentle Atli back in Bjarg.

The worst is to come. When Grettir returns to the family farm, he finds his father has also died and learns that Thorir has petitioned that year's Althing for him to be declared an outlaw. It is too late for him to offer any kind of defense; the sentence has already been passed.

After killing Atli's murderer and with an even higher price on his head, Grettir is forced to spend many years on the run, often in disguise, relying on old friends and kind strangers since his fear of the dark makes it difficult for him to endure hiding in the wilderness. He spends several years in a glacier-lined valley ruled by a friendly giant and his daughters, but eventually, he becomes restless. He knows Thorir will not give up his quest for revenge and will send assassins to hunt him down.

He hears about a lady called Steinvör who is being plagued by a malevolent troll that has taken her husband and his servant. Introducing himself as Gestur, Grettir offers to help and remains at her estate while she attends Yuletide Mass. When she fears she cannot go because the river is too high, Grettir carries her and her daughter over his left shoulder and crosses the raging torrent, pushing away great lumps of ice with his right arm.

Once they are safely on the other side, Grettir returns to the house and prepares to fight the trolls. As he waits, the doors fly open. A huge troll woman enters, eyes blazing. When she sees Grettir, she attacks. The two of them fight hard all night, leaving a trail of destruction behind them. The troll woman drags Grettir out of the house to a deep gulley by a waterfall, where, exhausted, he wildly swings his sword in a final attempt to stop her from dragging him in. Grettir cuts off her arm. She falls backward into the gulley and disappears.

After returning to the farmhouse, he and another man go to see if they can find Steinvör's husband, who might be in a cave behind the waterfall. His companion holds onto a rope while Grettir abseils down the cliff face.

Grettir dives into the deep gulley behind the waterfall and enters the cave. There, he finds a large fire with a giant stretched out beside it. As soon as the giant sees Grettir, he jumps up and snatches a wooden staff. Grettir manages to defend himself with his sword. When the giant reaches for a better weapon, Grettir slashes at his body and leaves a wound so deep and large that the giant's bowels fall out of his body and into the river.

When Grettir's waiting companion sees the bloody entrails being carried downstream, he believes they must be Grettir's and goes back to the farm to tell Steinvör of his death. Meanwhile, Grettir finishes off the stricken giant and then creeps farther into the cave, where he finds the bones of two men and a great deal of treasure. He puts them in a bag and makes his way to the bottom of the cliff. Since no one is there to help him, he is forced to haul himself up the rock face.

He reveals his true identity to Steinvör and hands her the remains of her husband and his servant and the treasure. She gives him a home until Grettir hears that Thorir's men are closing in on him. He goes back to Bjarg for the last time to tell his mother he is going to Drangey, a fortress on an island at the northern tip of Iceland. It is uninhabited and surrounded by cliffs. Drangey is only accessible by ladder.

Grettir's fifteen-year-old brother Illugi decides to go with him, but their mother knows it will end badly for both of them. They arrive at Drangey with another companion, Glaum, and make themselves at home. However, the families that own the island are far from pleased. They elect Thorbjörn Angle to get them to leave, and he makes several attempts to do this.

By this time, Grettir has been an outlaw for nineteen years. When the Althing decrees that he will soon be free since no man can be an outlaw for more than twenty years, Thorbjörn Angle is ordered to get rid of him before then, or he will lose his share of Drangey.

Thorbjörn consults his foster mother, Thurid, who is a witch, and she agrees to go with him to persuade Grettir to leave. However, when she starts to curse him, Grettir throws a rock at her that breaks her leg. Furious, she is forced to use her dark powers. She finds a tree trunk and carves blood runes into it before setting it out to sea.

On the island, Grettir sees this log a few times. He is suspicious of it, though, and doesn't bring it ashore. Glaum, however, doesn't realize and thinks it will make good firewood. When Grettir tries to cut it for firewood, the ax bounces off it and hacks into his leg.

The wound itself is compounded by the witch's blood runes, and Grettir grows weaker as Thorbjörn and his men storm the island. Glaum, who has already proved a liability, has forgotten to lift the ladder.

Illugi fights like a Trojan, but he can't fight them all. When Thorbjörn reaches Grettir, he finds he has succumbed to his cursed wound. The great, if unfortunate, warrior has died.

Thorbjörn kills Illugi in the hope of preventing a revenge killing and takes Grettir's head to make his claim for the bounty that Thorir had promised. However, when it becomes evident that his death was due to witchcraft, Thorir refuses to pay.

The long saga doesn't end with Grettir's death. His half-brother Thorsteinn Dromund (his father's son with his first wife, Rannveig of Tunsberg in Norway) begins a quest to avenge him, but the action moves from the Viking realms to Constantinople.

Chapter Three – A Guide to Norse Deities

The medieval people of Scandinavia put their faith in a complex system of deities that had various responsibilities over the different aspects of people's lives. Unfortunately for historians and scholars, contemporary Norse-written accounts are practically non-existent. Viking culture passed their history and stories down orally. Decisions, information, and deals were passed along and made by word of mouth. This system worked well since a Norseman's or Norsewoman's word was their bond.

In 98 CE, Roman general Tacitus wrote *Germania*, his study of the culture and customs of northern Europe that gives the earliest account of what has come to be known as Viking (or Norse) mythology. Through Roman trade with Scandinavia, he understood that these people worshiped a pantheon of gods and goddesses, some of whom could be compared to Roman deities.

Tacitus noted that Odin (Woden) was the main god and that animal and human sacrifices were made to him on a particular day of the week, Woden's day, which would become Wednesday. Similarly, Thor (or possibly the god Tyr) was worshiped on Thursday, and Frigg (or Freyja) was worshiped on Friday.

Around this time, the first discovered runestones were being crafted. The Futhark characters were generally used to commemorate and record heroic details about the lives of the great and the good in Norse societies. However, most of the runestones were carved around the time of Scandinavia's transition to Christianity and thus pay homage to Jesus and the Virgin Mary rather than Odin and Freyja. There are a small number of pagan stones that give a little insight into the old religion.

Modern understanding of Viking mythology chiefly relies on two books: the *Prose Edda* and the *Poetic Edda*. Since Scandinavia was almost exclusively Christian at the time these texts were compiled, the stories had evolved and become intertwined with biblical stories and messages, as well as a scattering of other pagan myths. (In the prologue to the *Prose Edda*, for example, the Norse gods are connected with the surviving heroes at the fall of Troy.)

The title page of a later edition of the Prose Edda.
https://commons.wikimedia.org/wiki/File:Edda.jpg

The *Prose Edda* was written by the Icelandic historian and politician Snorri Sturluson, probably in 1222 or 1223, as a reference to help young poets understand the complex meters of early skaldic poetry and the myths from the Scandinavian oral tradition. It consists of a prologue and three parts. In the *Gylfaginning* ("The Beguiling of Gylfi"), he describes Gylfi, a king of Sweden, visiting Asgard to question the gods. They explain their creation, many of their exploits, and the prophecy of the end of days known as *Ragnarök* ("Twilight of the Gods").

Although the *Prose Edda* is the most valuable resource, at the time of its writing, Snorri was engaged in an attempt to unify Iceland and Norway under the rule of King Haakon IV Haakonsson. Certain passages in the *Prose Edda* could be seen as an attempt to gain hearts and minds with a common cultural identity.

The *Poetic Edda* was written in the second half of the 13th century. It is a collection of mythological poetry composed throughout the Viking Age. None of the poems are attributed to an author, and it is believed that it is an anthology. Several versions still remain, including the treasured *Codex Regius*, which includes thirty-one poems.

These sources provide the stories of many Norse gods and goddesses whom the Vikings trusted for guidance and their well-being. As well as overseeing the lives of men and women, these mystical beings had their own trials and tribulations to deal with. Some of the most common themes include grueling searches for wisdom, the paramount value of honor and heroism, and coping with or executing theft and trickery.

There were three clans, houses, or races of these higher beings. Although they descended from the same ancestors and had inter-clan relationships, they were markedly different in their values and societies. They frequently clashed and even waged wars against each other.

The central, dominant pantheon (at least to humankind) was the Æsir in Asgard. The Æsir were gods and goddesses with the qualities to provide inspiration, comfort, and awe to the Vikings who revered them.

The Æsir

The Æsir are sometimes known as the sky gods. They are the higher pantheon of gods and goddesses in Viking mythology, and they reside in Asgard. They are immortal as long as they continue eating golden apples kept by Idunn, the goddess of spring, youth, and rejuvenation. When she was abducted along with her precious basket of apples by the jötun named Thiazzi, the inhabitants of Asgard aged and grew grey until she was rescued and returned to her orchard. Unlike deities in other polytheistic religions, Norse deities can be killed.

These Æsir gods and goddesses possess the qualities admired and valued by the Vikings, and their flaws and frailties could, for the most part, be identified with, accepted, or understood by the average person. The Æsir are associated with human qualities and concerns like war, strength, and society. There are many more named Æsir gods and goddesses than in the second pantheon, the Vanir, or the Jötun frost giants.

The principal Æsir god in Norse mythology was Odin (also known as Wōden in Old English, Wuotan in Old High German, and Wuodan in Old Dutch). The "All-Father" is the god of war and the dead. He is also the god of wisdom, poetry, and magic. He is the central figure in the Viking faith and rules over Valhalla, where the souls of great warriors are welcomed after they die. In his pursuit of knowledge, Odin frequently gains lovers with whom he fathers children.

Frigg, his ever-patient wife, is the queen of the Æsir and the benevolent goddess of motherhood. She is the mother of Baldr, Hod, and Hermod. In his work, Snorri suggests that Frigg is not averse to the odd extramarital affair. In the *Ynglinga Saga*, when Odin was absent from Asgard, he left his brothers, Vili and Vé, to rule in his stead. During that time, they regularly slept with Frigg.

Thor (Germanic for "thunder"), the son of Odin and the jötun goddess Jörð, is the mighty, hammer-wielding god of lightning and thunder. A fierce warrior, he is resilient and powerful. With the help of Mjölnir, his enchanted hammer, he is even able to fly. In some of the myths, he is susceptible to trickery and has been prosaically described as a "bonehead." However, these stories provide humor and a sense that at least one of the Æsir is not so different from humankind. Thus, he is regarded as a friend to man.

Sif, Thor's wife, is a goddess of the earth and family. She is known for her beauty and, in particular, her wonderful golden hair. Her son Ullr (Thor's stepson) is a particularly handsome god associated with skiing and winter. Sif and Thor's daughter Thrúd ("strength") is the goddess of battle. Modi ("wrath"), their son, is the god of wrath and was closely connected with the fearsome and ferocious Norse warriors known as berserkers. Magni ("mighty"), Thor's son by the jötun Járnsaxa ("Iron Dagger"), is a great warrior.

Thor's half-brother, the divine, Galahad-like Baldr ("prince"), is not as easy to relate to with his innate goodness, light, and unceasing joy. Nanna ("mother"), his wife, is associated with motherhood and is devoted to her wonderful husband. In some Danish myths, she was originally human and the lover of Baldr's blind brother Hodr ("warrior"). Nanna's sister, the gentle Lofn ("comforter"), is the goddess of forbidden love, adultery, and secret marriages, permitted by Odin and Frigg to bless marriages that have been banned. Another sister, the faithful Snotra ("clever"), serves Frigg and is associated with self-discipline and caution. The fourth sister, Sigyn ("friend of victory"), is the long-suffering wife of Loki and mother to Narfi and Váli. She is the goddess of kindness, patience, and devotion.

Other goddesses include Eir ("mercy"), who oversees medicine and childbirth and lives with her healers on Lyfjaberg, a hill where they await human *blót* offerings in exchange for their attention. Gefjun ("generous one") is a goddess of agriculture, particularly the harvest, and Syn ("refusal") is another handmaiden of Frigg. She is associated with rejection, refusal, and enforcing boundaries.

Fulla ("plenitude"), who also waits on Frigg and is responsible for her jewelry and footwear, is the goddess of secrets. The *Prose Edda* recounts that Sjöfn, the goddess of affection and friendship, is another dedicated companion of Frigg. Hlin (Old Norse for "protector") is often depicted with a sword and shield. She provides sanctuary for those Frigg decides to save and is the goddess of compassion, solace, and support. Gná, the goddess of wind transition and change, serves as Frigg's messenger and rides the flying horse Hófvarpnir ("Hoof-thrower") over the seas.

Tyr, another of Odin's sons, is the god of justice and resolution, while the goddess Var is responsible for overseeing promises and agreements with the power to punish those who break their oaths. Forseti, the son of Baldr and Nanna, is the god of peaceful negotiations. He supposedly had a courthouse in which he settled disputes with a flourish of his golden ax. The god Bragi is Asgard's wordsmith and poet. He is the husband of Idunn.

The Vanir

The Vanir gods and goddesses hail from Vanaheimr, a natural world of infinite beauty. It is a world of green woodlands and expanses of clear, calm waters. The Vanir are chiefly associated with fertility and magic. The Vanir women practice *seidhr* (also spelled as *seiðr* or seidr), a spiritual means of healing and prophecy capable of influencing the future. The Vanir are ethereal, introspective beings. Because there are fewer known Vanir deities than those of the Æsir, it is possible most of their stories have been forever lost.

Although the houses of the Æsir and Vanir exist peacefully alongside one another, this was not always the case. There was a long period of war that started when the Vanir goddess Gullveig visited Asgard. Odin and some of the other gods took an intense dislike to her because she cared for nothing but gold and riches. After a while, they became so sickened by her that they attacked her with spears and then threw her onto the fire. After it seemed she had burned away to nothing, she stepped out of the flames, reborn. So, they tried to burn her again, but the same thing happened. She survived a third fire, and that was enough for the Æsir to believe she had powers of witchcraft.

The Vanir gods and goddesses were, unsurprisingly, appalled at this treatment of one of their own and swore vengeance on the Æsir. Odin, from his all-seeing throne (Hlidskjalf), saw that the Vanir were preparing to fight, so he aimed his spear at them. This was the start of the first war of the world, at least according to the Vikings.

The Vanir used magic and spells to fight against the Æsir, who counterattacked with weapons. After a long time, it became clear that neither side was close to victory, so the leaders met to try and work out the way forward. After arguing about the origins of the war, airing their grievances about the various methods employed, and claiming they were due reparations, the two groups agreed that it would be better for the two houses to integrate so they could live peaceably and unified. Two of the Vanir leaders, Njörd and his son Freyr, came to Asgard. They were accompanied by Njörd's daughter Freyja. The Æsir sent the wisest of their gods, Mímir ("the rememberer" or "the wise one") and Hœnir to Vanaheimr.

To seal the end of the Æsir-Vanir War, each of the gods and goddesses spat into a pot in a solemn gesture to bond the two houses. This created the god of poetry, diplomacy, and inspiration: Kvasir. Although he was just as much an Æsir, he is more associated with the Vanir, perhaps because of his otherworldliness and his propensity to wander and roam while sharing his wisdom.

Initially, the Vanir welcomed their Æsir representatives. They even made Hœnir one of their leaders. However, since he always deferred to the wise Mímir, they grew suspicious and thought perhaps the Æsir had tricked them. When their doubts turned to anger, they seized Mímir and sliced off his head. They sent the head to Odin. The wise god wrapped the head in special herbs and spoke charms to it until it was enchanted enough to speak with him and share his secrets.

Njörd ("force" or "power") was the god of the sea, fishing, and mild weather. According to the *Ynglinga Saga*, he married his own (unnamed) sister, who became the mother of his two children. After his second marriage to the jötun maiden Skadi ("shadow"), the couple left Asgard to live at Skadi's father's hall in the snowy mountains. It only took nine nights for Njörd to realize he could not bear the bleak, endless winters and the howling wolves. So, they returned to his lakeside hall of Noatun. Skadi found it just as difficult to settle there, so after another nine days, they agreed to part. Skadi-a goddess associated with skiing-later became one of Odin's lovers.

Freyja ("lady") is the iconic Viking female deity associated with fertility, beauty, love, and war. She welcomes the ordinary soldiers killed in battle to her hall, Fólkvangr, where they can enjoy the lovely and serene surroundings while the warlords and heroes feast at Valhalla. She is not typically depicted with a weapon, but she possesses *fjaðrhamr*, a marvelous cloak made from falcon feathers that allows the wearer to fly or shapeshift into the form of a falcon.

Since Freyja is the goddess of free love and promiscuousness, she is said to have had relations with every god, including her brother. Her husband, the Vanir god Ódr, is associated with recklessness and madness. He prefers to live a lonely life, wandering from place to place, much to his wife's chagrin. Freyja spends much of her time searching for him in disguise while weeping tears of gold. They share two daughters: Hnoss ("jewel"), a goddess of lust and desire, and Gersemi ("treasure"), associated with adornment, cherished items, and friendship.

Freyja's brother and her twin (at least in some accounts) is Freyr ("lord"), the god of sunny weather, prosperity, and fertility. He is thought to be one of the most popular Viking gods; there are a lot of artifacts that bear his likeness. From Odin's high seat, Hlidskjalf, Freyr sees and falls in love with the jötun Gerd. Determined to win her hand, he presents her with some of Idunn's apples as a gift. Eventually, she marries him, but only after he has given away his enchanted sword that can fight on its own. The *Ynglinga Saga* recounts that their son, Fjölnir, became an ancient king of Sweden.

Freyr rides a golden boar that can be seen in the dark. This animal is named Gullinbursti ("golden bristles"). He also has a magical ship that will always find a favorable wind for its sails and needs no mooring since it can be folded up to fit in his pocket. He also has three loyal servants called Skírnir, Byggvir, and Beyla.

Nerthus is another Vanir goddess associated with fertility and regrowth. It is possible that she is the sister of Njörd (and the mother of Freyr and Freyja), but this is by no means certain. Her story is mysterious and vague, but it is known that early northern European tribes held her in great esteem. They would include a wagon draped in white dedicated to her in a traveling procession.

Gullveig ("gold drunk" in Old Norse), whose torture was the cause of the Æsir-Vanir War, is a Vanir sorceress, seer, and goddess of gold and precious metals.

The Jötnar

Jötunheim is traditionally the home of a great tribe (or tribes) called the jötnar (singular jötun). They have superhuman strength and are sometimes described as frost giants, though in other legends, they are described as being of a similar height to humans. (There were some marriages between the inhabitants of Asgard and those of Jötunheim, so it is generally assumed they were of a similar height/species.) Their realm is described as a wintry, remote wilderness with high mountains and dense, inhospitable forests that echo with the howls of wolves.

In the earlier accounts, the jötnar are often very wise and intelligent but have different values than the Æsir and Vanir. Likely because of the influence of Christianity, they developed into hideous and monstrous creatures that were malevolent but often easy to outwit. Over time, many folklorists believe the concept of the jötnar evolved into mountain-dwelling Scandinavian trolls, which are staples of many modern fairytales.

Some of the early jötnar were very beautiful, such as Gerd, the wife of the Vanir god Freyr. In *Skírnismál* (a poem in the *Poetic Edda*), Gerd is described as remarkably lovely, her beauty illuminating the air and seas. After her marriage, she became one of Asgard's goddesses, representing fertility and earthly love. Hrodr, the friendly giantess, wife of Hymir, the trusted friend of Odin and Thor, and (in some stories) the mother of Tyr, is another attractive jötun. Vor (or Vörr), the handmaiden of Frigg, was originally from Jötunheim. Before the Æsir-Vanir War, she was one of Odin's confidants and provided some helpful advice. After she pledged her allegiance to the Æsir, she became the goddess of truth and prophecy.

Beli ("roarer") is Gerd's brother. In *Gylfaginning*, Freyr is forced to fight him to gain Gerd's hand. However, he has to fight Beli without any weapon since he already gave his sword away. Freyr eventually manages to kill Beli with a stag antler.

Thrym is named the powerful king of Jötunheim. He is the ice giant god of cold and ice. In a humorous story about Thor, the mighty god of thunder, attempting to recover his hammer that Thrym has stolen (or found), Thrym's magnificent hall is described, as is the magnificent feast awaiting his guests.

Ægir, the jötun god of the sea and brewing, is a generous host at the great banquets held in his magnificent palace underneath the sea. These feasts are attended and enjoyed by the gods of the Æsir. His wife, the jötun goddess Rán, also personifies the sea but is far more sinister, cruel, and unwelcoming. She is reputed to lure sailors to their deaths with an enchanted net she uses to drag them beneath the waves. In some of the Icelandic myths, she hosts her own feasts for those drowned at sea as long as they are able to pay their way. It eventually became the custom for Vikings to ensure they carried some gold while they were at sea so they could pay Rán if necessary. Ægir and Rán share a son, Snær, the god of snow, and nine daughters, the waves of the sea. These are generally considered to be the collective mothers of the emerald-toothed god Heimdallr, whose father is Odin. Heimdallr (or Heimdall) was gifted with foresight and tasked with the vital role of guarding the enchanted rainbow bridge called Bifröst.

The jötnar are not so much enemies of the gods of the Æsir as they are allies.; In Asgard, the deities strive to create order and clarity for themselves and humankind. Inevitably, there are clashes and conflicts from time to time, which are not always the fault of the jötnar. However, it is important to remember that there were several relationships and marriages between them, most of which led to children.

Chapter Four – The Norse Cosmos: The Dawn of Time

According to the Vikings' religion, in the beginning-before life itself-there was nothing. This empty, yawning void (according to *Grímnismál* in the *Poetic Edda)* was known as Ginnungagap. To the north of this dark expanse of nothingness, a fountain or well eventually emerged called Hvergelmir. Its waters provided the means for the growth of Yggdrasil, the colossal ash tree.

Ash was a tree well known to the Vikings. It is quick to grow with sufficient water and can mature into a tall tree within a decade. Its timber was used by Norse shipbuilders and woodworkers. Ash wood is flexible, shock resistant, and tends not to split, so this species of tree was the natural choice for Yggdrasil, the world tree.

An illustration of Yggdrasil.

Yggdrasil's roots extended deep into the very depths of Ginnungagap, eventually reaching the Well of Urd, where the three Norns (or Nornir) reside. The Norns are described in *Völuspá* (the best-known poem in the *Poetic Edda*) as being Urd (the past), Verdandi (the present), and Skuld(the future). These three Jötnar sisters have the power to influence fate. Urd, the oldest, is a wizened old woman who always looks to the past. Verdandi is young and looks straight ahead with a strong and steady gaze. These two sisters weave destiny together while Skuld, the most frightening and who is completely veiled, periodically rips apart their weaving, throwing the cosmos into chaos and confusion. The three of them also carve runes into Yggdrasil that foretell the future.

In *Grímnismál,* Yggdrasil is imagined differently. It has three great roots:

"'Neath the first lives Hel,

'Neath the second the frost giants,

'Neath the last are the lands of men."[2]

Each of the three roots took water from its own well: Urðarbrunnr tended by the Norns, the creation waters of Hvergelmir, and Mímisbrunnr, the well of wisdom.

At the base of Yggdrasil, several snakes evolve and slither around with the dragon, Níðhöggr (or Nidhogg), who bites and chews at the roots to cause damage to the tree.

The excess waters that flowed from Hvergelmir formed the icy, misty realm of Niflheim and eleven rivers of freezing cold water collectively called Élivágar. At the same time, the southern part of Ginnungagap began to grow increasingly warmer until it became Muspelheim, a fiery furnace of flames, thick black smoke, and lava.

This raging heat began to warm the barren, frozen wasteland of Niflheim until small droplets of thawed water fell. As they fell on Muspelheim, they created sparks that flew into the darkness to create stars.

As the fire and ice began to join together, they created a ball of energy that resulted in the creation of the first being, Ymir ("screamer"), a jötun. An alternative version of this myth is that the sparks wielded by the flaming sword of the fire giant Surtr ("the swarthy one") created the celestial bodies and brought about the conditions for Ymir's creation.

In another version of this story, from *Gylfaginning* in the *Prose Edda,* Ymir is not a product of the merging of the elements but was born of the "yeasty" venom called *eitr,* found in the waters of Élivágar:

"Down from Élivágar did venom drop,

And waxed till a giant it was;

And thence arose our giant's race,

And thus so fierce are we found."[3]

---

[2] *The Poetic Edda.* Translated by Carolyne Larrington. Snorri Sturluson. Oxford University Press, 2014.

At the same time, the immense primordial cow Audhumla (Auðumla, "destroyer of deserts") was created. The *Gylfaginning* explains that this hornless cow, similar to those that northern European farmers had bred since prehistoric times, provided four rivers of milk that fed Ymir while she licked the rime from the surface ice for her own sustenance.

Suitably fed, Ymir rested. From each of his armpits came a male and a female being. His legs created a six-headed monster. These were the ancestors of the jötnar.

Meanwhile, as Audhumla lapped at the ice, her warm tongue made it thaw. On the first day, she uncovered the hair of the first god, which had formed beneath the ice. On the second day, his head was revealed, and on the third day, his body could be seen. His name was Búri ("producer"). He was the first of the Æsir and was (according to the *Gylfaginning*) "fair of feature, great and mighty." Thus, Audhumla had an essential role in the formation of both the Æsir and the jötnar.

Búri had a son (by means unknown or unexplained) called Borr ("borer"). While dreaming, Búri had a vision that the jötnar were evil, so he and his son set about ridding the world of Ymir and his descendants. However, as each night fell, the fighting ended without either side achieving a victory over the other.

Borr married a jötun named Bestla ("wife"), the daughter of the giant Bölthorn ("evil- thorn"). They had three sons: Odin, Vili ("will), and Vé ("wish"). Together, the brothers killed Ymir (their maternal great-grandfather) after finally beating their enemy in battle. So much blood poured from the old giant's wounds that all of the jötnar drowned in it, with the exception of Bergelmir ("mountain-yeller"), who would become the ancestor of the future generations of frost giants.

Odin, Vili, and Vé then took Ymir's remains to the center of Ginnungagap to create the world. In the poem *Grímnismál*, Odin recalls how Ymir's blood became the seas; his bones became hills and mountains; his teeth became rocks, stones, and gravel; his muscle and skin sand and gravel; and his hair the trees.

The brothers took his skull and placed it over the world to form the heavens. Four dwarves named Nordri, Sudri, Austri, and Vestri (the compass directions are taken from these four) took the four corners and

---

[3] *The Prose Edda—Tales from Norse Mythology.* Translated by Jesse Byock. Snorri Sturluson. Penguin Classics, 2005.

held it aloft. They captured some of the sparks flying from the swirling furnace of Muspelheim and threw them into the newly created skies and created the sun, moon, and stars so that their new world was no longer veiled in darkness.

Fearing the jötnar might approach this realm with evil intent, Odin, Vili, and Vé took Ymir's eyebrows and formed them into a boundary to encircle the world and keep it safe.

Once they were satisfied their work was complete, the brothers set about creating the first people to live there. They carved a man and a woman from two tree trunks they found lying on the beach. Odin breathed life into them. Vili gave them blood and the ability to see, hear, speak, and reason, as well as a healthy complexion. Not to be outdone, Vé gave them suitable clothing.

However, in the *Poetic Edda*, Odin, Hœnir, and Lódurr found the already-created humans wandering around with no sense or means of understanding. Odin gave them their mental capacity, Hœnir gave them blood, and Lódurr sorted out their complexions. Since Hœnir and Lódurr are not mentioned again and so little is known of them, the first account (the *Prose Edda*) is the version that is generally preferred.

The brothers named the man Ask (Old Norse for "ash tree") and the woman Embla ("elm" or perhaps "water pot" or "vine"). The humans started a peaceful life on the newly created Midgard. After they had spent some time wandering around and exploring their habitat, they found a dwelling already built and waiting for them. They settled down there and tamed the more biddable animals. They also had several children.

As Midgard became more populated with their perfect descendants, Odin made Ask and Embla rulers of the realm. As the years passed, the jötnar, elves, and other beings came to Midgard disguised as humans and had children with the native people. Later generations were corrupted by the cruelty and evilness associated with those beings.

The story of the creation of the sun and moon and the explanation of their movement is accounted for in the *Gylfaginning*. Gylfi, an ancient king of Sweden who traveled to Asgard on a quest for knowledge, met with Hárr ("high"), Jafnhárr ("just as high"), and Thridi ("third"), mystical beings of the Æsir. It is possible these three deities were Odin and his brothers Vili and Vé, but they could also all have been Odin. King Gylfi learns that the sun races through the sky because a savage wolf, Sköll, is in pursuit, ready to devour it. Similarly, the moon is being hunted by another wolf, Hati.

The Wolves Pursuing Sol and Mani.
https://commons.wikimedia.org/wiki/File:The_Wolves_Pursuing_Sol_and_Mani.jpg

These monsters are the sons of a giantess named Hródvitnir, who lives far to the east of Midgard and has given birth to many wolf-like giants. In other accounts, Sköll ("shadow") and Hati ("hatred") are the sons of Fenrir (the son of Loki and the giantess Angrboda). They were born in the Járnvidr ("iron-wood") forest. Since their mother might also have been their paternal grandmother, this lineage might explain their frenzied bloodlust.

The sun and moon deities, Sól and Máni, respectively, were originally human, according to the *Poetic Edda*. When their father, Mundilfari, arrogantly named them after the revered celestial bodies, the Æsir had them banished to the skies. In a more charitable version, the Æsir appreciated their beauty and gave them the great honor of serving the gods.

These two siblings were given the unenviable task of guiding the sun and moon across the sky each day. Sól pulls the sun in a chariot drawn by two horses named Árvakr ("swift") and Álsvidr ("early riser"). Traveling alongside her in the chariot is a man called Svalinn, who holds a shield aloft to protect the people of Midgard from the strength of the sun's rays.

In the *Gylfaginning*, Máni "guides the path of the moon and controls its waxing and waning." He is followed by two younger children, Hjúki ("the one coming to strength") and Bil ("the waning one"), who had been fetching water from the Byrgir well. These two are almost certainly the origin of Jack and Jill of nursery rhyme fame.

The Norse creation myths share several concepts with other cultures. The central, all-important Yggdrasil is similar to the sacred fig tree Aśvattha in Hindu scriptures, the sacred *Erica* tree in which the body of Osiris is held in Egyptian mythology, and the Bodhi (banyan) tree that brought enlightenment to Buddha. There is also the Tree of Life in the Garden of Eden. Also, sacred cow deities like Audhumla are seen in ancient Egyptian myths (such as the goddess Hathor) and in Hinduism as Kamadhenu, the Divine Mother. The story of the two first male and female progenitors is the basis of most religions and creation myths throughout world history.

Of course, we must remember the written sources we depend on for Norse myths (including the *Poetic Edda* and the *Prose Edda*) were produced well after the spread of Christianity, so some of these stories are likely quite different from the original versions.

Chapter Five – Yggdrasil and the Nine Realms

The massive branches of the world tree Yggdrasil, dubbed the "noblest of trees" by Odin in the *Grímnismál*, reached high and wide. A giant eagle is perched at the tree's very uppermost point. On the eagle's beak and between its eyes sits the hawk, Vedrfölnir ("storm pale"). Together, they keep watch over the nine realms of the Norse cosmos.

The dreadful dragon Nidhogg, coiling around Yggdrasil's roots, sends a squirrel named Ratatoskr ("the traveler") to deliver horrible insults to the eagle, which extends its wings and flaps them in anger, causing the tree to shake. The eagle sends inflammatory messages back to Nidhogg, agitating him so that he writhes in fury. This helps to explain conditions like gale-force winds (from the eagle's wings) and earth tremors (from the movement of the snake). In the poem *Grímnismál* in the *Poetic Edda*, Odin reveals there are more snakes "than any unwise ape can imagine" living beneath the roots of Yggdrasil and that the old tree "suffers agony more than men know" as it endures the snakes' venom and the endless gnawing of its bark by four stags named Daínn, Dvalinn, Duneyrr, and Duraþrór.

The three Norns, as well as weaving the destinies of all beings, tend to the tree and bathe any damage and wounds to it with waters from their sacred well of Urðarbrunnr ("well of fates"). In his quest to gain wisdom, Odin visits the Norns to try to understand their knowledge and learn from their runes, the powerful symbols that make up the sacred ancient

Germanic alphabet that hold the secrets and mysteries of the universe. In Skaldic poetry, these runes hold the key to wielding magic.

The Norns carve the fate of all beings into the roots of Yggdrasil using the sacred rune alphabet. As Odin watches them work, he becomes more and more envious of the power and knowledge they possess. When he begs them to share their wisdom, the Norns tell him that they will only reveal themselves to one who is worthy. So, Odin is forced to take drastic action to gain the mystical knowledge he craves.

After impaling himself with his spear, he hangs himself from the branches of Yggdrasil for nine days, insisting that no one must help him or bring him food. For nine days, he stares at the runes and awaits enlightenment. In the poem *Hávamál*, he recalls:

> "I ween that I hung on the windy tree,
>
> Hung there for nine nights full nine; and offered I was,
>
> To Odin, myself to myself,
>
> On the tree that none may know
>
> What root beneath it runs.
>
> None made me happy with a loaf or horn,
>
> And there below I looked;
>
> I took up the runes, shrieking I took them,
>
> And forthwith back I fell."

His sacrifice is successful. On the ninth day, the runes finally reveal themselves to him. Having understood them, he imparts the knowledge he has gained to others during his incessant wandering.

Upon the great tree Yggdrasil are nine realms, including the fortified human world that is Midgard. The concept of these realms is frequently reinforced in both the *Poetic Edda* and the *Prose Edda*, but they are never comprehensively listed or defined, so it has been left to scholars and mythologists to ascertain exactly what these realms were. Thus, there is some ambiguity. Allowing that there are some worlds that overlap and the mention of other possible worlds, it is widely accepted that the nine realms are Asgard, Vanaheimr, Álfheim, Midgard, Svartálfheim, Jötunheim, Niflheim, Muspelheim, and Helheim.

Asgard is the realm of the Æsir. According to the *Prose Edda*, it is in the center of the world and surrounded by Midgard, the human world, with Jötunheim beyond that, suggesting that the nine realms may have been some system of concentric discs with Yggdrasil as a kind of vertical axis at the center.

According to the *Völuspá*, Asgard suffered a great deal of damage during the war with the Vanir and had to be rebuilt. The *Grímnismál* from the *Poetic Edda* tells the story of a jötun disguised as a master builder (in some accounts, he gives his name as Borgarsmidr). He approaches the Æsir with an offer to rebuild Asgard over three winters in exchange for the sun, the moon, and the goddess Freyja. The gods agree, despite Freyja's absolute refusal to cooperate with any such bargain. However, the Æsir demand that it should be completed within a year, believing this impossible target would get Asgard rebuilt without the possibility of losing the celestial bodies and Freyja. The jötun accepts these terms and gets to work. His mighty stallion, Svadilfari ("unlucky traveler"), moves the great boulders to help him, and he works like a man possessed. It is soon clear that the builder is on schedule to finish within the year.

Horrified, the Æsir realize they will have to do something to slow his progress and call upon Loki, the trickster god and unofficial problem solver, for help. Loki, a shapeshifter, transforms himself into a pretty mare in the hope of distracting Svadilfari. The stallion quickly loses interest in helping his master. No longer able to rely on the horse's brute strength, the building slows down. When the builder realizes that he is doomed to fail, he loses his temper and reveals himself to be a jötun, an enemy of the Æsir. Thor swiftly kills him with his hammer, Mjölnir. In another version of this myth, the builder was employed to build a great fortified wall around Asgard rather than the citadel itself.

Loki seriously distracted Svadilfari and ended up bearing Sleipnir ("slippy one"), the eight-legged horse that could travel through the air and over water. It has also been suggested that the eight legs are reminiscent of the pallbearers that carry the dead, possibly since Loki gifted the horse to Odin, the god of the dead.

Odin and Sleipnir from an 18th-century Icelandic manuscript.
https://commons.wikimedia.org/wiki/File:Odin_riding_Sleipnir.jpg

Iðavöllr ("splendor plain"), mentioned twice in the *Völuspá*, is at the center of Asgard. There, "Shrines and temples they timbered high; Forges they set, and smithies ore, Tongs they wrought, and tools they fashioned." There is Gladsheimr ("bright home"), which, according to *Gylfaginning*, is a meeting place for the Æsir with thirteen high seats where the gods meet to hold council–perhaps a little reminiscent of King Arthur's Round Table in Old English mythology. In the *Gylfaginning*, it is described as "a temple in which there were seats for the twelve of them, apart from the high seat of the All-father. This is the largest and best dwelling on earth; outside and in it is like pure gold." Vingólf, "a very beautiful building," is the hall and meeting place of the goddesses of Asgard. It is also on that plain. Baldr's hall, Breidablik, is the most beautiful of the god's dwellings: *Gylfaginning* states "in that place may nothing unclean be." Baldr and Nanna's son, Forseti, the god of justice, has his own silver and golden hall called Glitnir ("shining one"), which is also used as a courthouse for the Æsir.

Asgard is also home to Odin's great hall, Valhalla, and Freyja's hall, Sessrúmnir, where the souls of human heroes and warriors reside. There are several other halls and dwellings in Asgard. Odin himself has several halls. The Valaskjálf ("shelf of the slain") has a shining silver roof and a tall tower in which Odin has his throne that allows him to see over all nine realms.

Thor's hall, Bilskirnir, is described as the largest in all of the nine realms and has more than 540 rooms. The second largest hall is Landvidi, the hall of the god Vídar. He lives there with his mother Gridr. It is unkempt and overgrown with wild grasses. The god of archery, Ullr, has a home near the forest of Ýdalir ("yew dales"), where he can go to collect the best branches for his bows and arrows.

The queen of the Æsir, Odin's wife Frigg, has a hall named Fensalir ("Fen Halls") in the wetlands of Asgard. Njörd, the Vanir god who made his home in Asgard after the peace agreement, has a hall called Noatun ("place of the ships") at the edge of the sea. There, he watches over sailors and fishermen. Sökkvabekkr ("sunken benches"), the hall of Saga, the hospitable goddess of second sight, is a place "where cool waves flow, And amid their murmur it stands; there daily do Odin and Saga drink, In gladness from cups of gold."[4]

Between Asgard and Midgard is the Bifröst, an enchanted burning rainbow bridge that stretches from Asgard to the human realm Midgard. According to *Grímnismál*, Heimdallr, guardian of the bridge and a god who requires less sleep than a bird, has "his well built house" there.

In the *Prose Edda* (specifically, the *Gylfaginning*), there is more information about the Bifröst. It was built by the gods "with art and skill to a greater extent than other constructions" and consists of three colors.

---

[4] *The Poetic Edda.* Translated by Carolyne Larrington. Snorri Sturluson. Oxford University Press, 2014.

Every day, the gods ride their horses across it, apart from Thor, who wades through the boiling waters of the river Körmt to reach Urðarbrunnr, where they discuss the order of the day.

The realm of the Vanir, Vanaheimr, is not described in any great detail in the Eddas. It is thought to be a temperate and lush, rather overgrown, forest world, a place that is more natural than the ordered city of Asgard. In *Lokasenna* of the *Poetic Edda,* Loki states that the Vanir god Njörd came eastward to Asgard, which would indicate that the realm of Vanaheimr is positioned somewhere to the west.

The third realm on the highest level of the cosmos is Álfheim ("home of the elves"), also called Ljósálfheimr or Álfheimr. It is home to the Ljósálfar ("light elves"). These beings are closely associated with the Vanir and are "more beautiful than the sun," according to the *Prose Edda.* The god Freyr rules over Álfheim; it was given to him as a gift when he was a child.

Midgard ("middle enclosure") is the realm of humans. It was created by Odin and his brothers from the body of the giant Ymir. It is the world between the heavenly, ordered realms and those of evil and chaos.

The svartálfar ("swarthy elves"), sometimes known as dökkálfar ("dark elves"), inhabit Svartálfheim ("home of the swarthy elves"), also known as Nidavellir or Myrkheim.[5] It is the realm of dwarves. It is a dark, bleak, and unwelcoming terrain, with clusters of underground caverns beneath twisted, gnarled roots. It is below Midgard and above Helheim on the World Tree.

Jötunheim ("world of giants") is the realm of the jötnar or frost giants. The descriptions paint a picture of immensely tall mountains and vast, dark forests. It is not a particularly hospitable place, at least for the Æsir, Vanir, or humans. It is sometimes referred to as Útgardr ("beyond the fence" or "outer enclosure"), which supports the theory of the realms being concentric circles with Yggdrasil as a central spindle. However, it has also been suggested that Útgardr is some kind of major settlement -a kind of capital city-of this realm.

Niflheim ("world of mist"), the first of the two primordial realms that existed before life began, is an icy, frozen land of mist and darkness where creation began. It is sometimes confused with Helheim, which the

---

[5] Most sources use svartálfar and dökkálfar interchangeably, but some sources state they are separate.

goddess Hel rules; in some sagas, they do overlap. It is inhabited by ancient ice giants that are presumably different than the jötnar in Jötunheim. It is generally considered a barren wilderness since most life cannot survive.

According to *Gylfaginning* in the *Prose Edda*, it is the location of the well of Hvergelmir, one of the springs at the roots of Yggdrasil, and the frozen rivers of Élivágar that were an important element in the beginning of life.

Muspelheim ("world destroyer"), the second primordial realm, is the domain of the fire giants or demons. Their chief, Surtr ("the swarthy one"), a terrifying giant, guards the border with a flaming sword. It is a smoky, glowing land of flames and volcanos where no one could survive other than the local inhabitants.

The ship *Naglfar*, mentioned in the *Poetic Edda* and *Prose Edda*, is made of dead peoples' untrimmed fingernails. Once it is complete, it will play a role in the final battle of Ragnarök. The character High sagely suggests that it is wise to keep one's nails short and tidy so that the ship will take longer to be built.

In this vein, according to the *Prose Edda*, Surtr will lead the fire giants in the final great battle during Ragnarök: "At the end of the world he will go and wage war and defeat all the gods and burn the whole world with fire." Just as it was a part of creation, Muspelheim is there for the destruction of life.

Helheim ("Hel's world"), at the very bowels of the cosmos, is ruled over by Loki's daughter Hel and is the final destination of the dead. It is said to lay downward and northward and is divided into several areas. Hel's hall is named Eljudnir (Éljúðnir) ("sprayed with snowstorms"). and is situated in Niflheim. Helheim is a bleak and icy landscape, battered by storms of hail and freezing winds. It has high, impenetrable walls. The dead must cross the golden bridge of Gjallarbrú over the river Gjöll to reach her hall. This bridge is guarded by a maniacal jötun giantess called Modgud ("war frenzy"), who decides who shall enter the gates of Eljudnir and prevents anyone from leaving.

Immediately outside the hall is Garm, a vicious and monstrous hound that guards the gates. There is also Fallandaforad, a great pitfall in which Hel has her bed, kör ("sickbed"), obscured by tattered curtains called Blikjandaböl ("gleaming disaster"). There, she is waited on by her servants, Ganglati and Ganglot (both names mean "lazy walker"), who move so slowly that it is hard to see whether they are actually moving at all. They bring her meals on a plate known as "hunger," and she eats it with the knife she calls "famine."

For the very worst sinners, Náströnd ("corpse beach") was their final destination. The souls of these murderers, adulterers, and oath-breakers were forced to wade through venom to a north-facing castle, its roof a mass of writhing snakes. There, they would suffer eternal torment, namely torture by the vile dragon Nidhogg, who sucks the blood from their bodies.

Chapter Six – Odin the All-Father

In Viking mythology, Odin is the god of wisdom, knowledge, poetry, runes, ecstasy, and magic, but he is primarily a war god and is responsible for those who die in battle. As the chief of the Æsir gods and goddesses, he is an extremely complex and multi-faceted character.

As a great warrior, he is said to have never lost a battle (although the end of the first war between the Æsir and Vanir was hardly a resounding victory). After he and his brother created Midgard, Odin traveled extensively throughout all nine realms, involving himself in many wars and battles. The Norse warriors believed that Odin would decide which side would defeat the other and prayed to him for protection and guidance. They made sacrifices to him before going into battle. The ferocious and fearless berserkers, who fought as though they were in a trance and disregarded the most severe wounds, considered him their patron. In Adam of Bremen's text, *Gesta Hammaburgensis ecclesiae pontificum* (*Deeds of the Bishops of Hamburg*), he refers to Odin as Wotan in his description of the Temple at Uppsala and describes him as the god of war to whom people would leave sacrifices during times of conflict.

Although Odin is indisputably the chief of the Norse gods, the *Ynglinga Saga* describes him as "king of the Æsir." Both Tacitus and Adam of Bremen state Thor was the primary god in the Norse pagan religion, so it may not be until the Eddas that Odin became the central father figure of Asgard. He is mentioned in most of the stories in the Eddas, but that could be a result of the influence of Christianity. Many of

Odin's experiences are comparable with figures from the Bible, including himself hanging from the world tree Yggdrasil, his contemplations in the wilderness, and his paternal attitude to the people of Midgard.

A 9th-century depiction of Odin.
https://commons.wikimedia.org/wiki/File:Ardre_Odin_Sleipnir.jpg

As well as being the creator, Odin is the father to several gods. Thor, Baldr, Vídar, and Váli are identified as his children in the Eddas. Heimdallr, Bragi, Tyr, Hodr, and Hermód have questionable parentage, and in some accounts, Odin is their father. He is also the founder of earthly dynasties, such as the Burgundian kings in the *Völsunga Saga*. Skjöldr, the legendary Danish king, and King Sæmingr of Norway were also said to be sons of Odin. In 2020, a haul of treasure was discovered in a field in Jelling, Denmark. It included a gold bracteate (pendant) weighing eight hundred grams that dates to the 5th century CE. It is inscribed in runic letters with the owner's name, "Jaga" or "Jagaz," thought to be a chieftain who might have claimed Odin as an ancestor with the words "Odin's man" alongside the image of a man and a horse.

The mother of Thor Odinson, Odin's oldest son, is generally attributed as the earth goddess Jörd. There is some confusion, however, since Jörd has also been listed as Odin's daughter. The goddess Frigg (Odin's wife) is said to be the daughter of Fjörgynn, another name for Jörd. Some of this confusion may have arisen from the name Jörd also being the Old Norse word for "earth."

Odin is described in *Gylfaginning* in the *Prose Edda* as "beloved of Frigg." As his wife, Frigg is queen of the Æsir, and she is the mother of their ill-fated children, Baldr and Hodr.

In one of the *Poetic Edda* myths, Agnar and Geirrod, the young sons of King Hraudung, are out fishing when their boat is blown ashore. A farmer and his wife (who are revealed to be Odin and Frigg) find them and look after them over the winter. The farmer takes a particular interest in Geirrod, while his wife cares for his older brother. The following spring, the old man gives them a boat, whispers something to his favorite foster son, and sends them on their way.

As they reach their home, Geirrod jumps out of the boat and pushes it back to sea with Agnar still aboard, cursing him. "Go wherever the trolls take you," he tells his brother. The enchanted boat sails swiftly away. As Geirrod enters his father's hall, he finds his father had died while he had been away. Since the older brother is lost at sea, Geirrod is crowned king.

One day, Odin is laughing at Agnar's fate while living in a cave with a troll woman and their children. Frigg points out that while Geirrod may be king, he is a bad ruler. He is mean and stingy. Geirrod will not feed his guests if there are too many of them, which is unforgivable behavior to the hospitable, feast-loving Vikings. Odin, unwilling to believe his foster son could be capable of such a heinous crime, makes a wager with Frigg that this simply isn't so. Odin prepares to go and see Geirrod for himself disguised as Grimnir ("shadowed face").

Frigg quickly sends her handmaiden Fulla to tell Geirrod that a malevolent sorcerer is on his way to his kingdom to cause harm but that he will be easy to recognize since no dog will bark at him. When Grimnir arrives, Geirrod sets his dogs on him (as he has done with all of his guests). When the dogs will not so much as sniff at the stranger, Geirrod orders his men to tie up Grimnir and suspend him between two large fires for eight nights in an attempt to make him reveal his intentions. Of course, the disguised god will not speak.

Geirrod's young son, also named Agnar (just like the brother the king had betrayed), takes pity on the prisoner and gives him a drink of mead. By that point, the fire has become so fierce that Odin's disguise has burned away. Odin begins to speak to the boy. He tells him about Asgard and the many names and disguises he has taken.

Agnar reveals the tortured prisoner's true identity to his father. Geirrod, horrified, leaps to his feet to go and free Odin from the fire, but in his haste, he falls upon his sword and is killed. Agnar (the son, not the brother) then becomes king and rules wisely for many years.

Odin is sometimes referred to as the "raven god." His association with these birds certainly predates the Eddas. Artifacts from the Viking Age often depict him with representations of ravens, and in folklore, it is said that their appearance after a sacrifice was a sign that Odin had accepted it. In the *Poetic Edda*'s *Grímnismál*, Odin speaks of his own ravens, Hugin (possibly from the Old Norse *hugr*, meaning "thought") and Munin (from *munr*, meaning "memory"). These ravens fly all over the world each day. When they return, they whisper to Odin, telling him all they have seen.

As well as his bird companions, Odin has two grey wolves, Freki ("the ravenous one") and Geri ("the greedy one"). It has been said that Odin created them for company when he felt lonely during his travels, and they became his loyal guardians. Vikings were encouraged to respect and learn from these animals. Ravens were known for their intelligence, and wolves were as courageous and wise. Wolves had a strong sense of family since they demonstrably took care of all members of their packs.

A great deal of Odin's time is spent in the pursuit of knowledge. In the *Poetic Edda*'s *Völuspá*, the wisest of all of the gods was initially Mímir, a mysterious water deity who lives at the Mimisbrunnr well that provides water for the Jötunheim root of Yggdrasil. (In other stories, wise Mímir was the unfortunate Vanir god whose decapitated head Odin carried with him.) According to the *Völuspá*, Mímir guards this well as it is where "wisdom and understanding were stored." Anyone who drank its waters would be forever enlightened. Mímir drinks from it every morning. When Odin visits, craving knowledge, he has to forfeit one of his eyes for a share.

Mímir pours the water into the Gjallarhorn, one of the Æsirs' most treasured possessions. As well as being a drinking horn, Gjallarhorn is also a musical instrument. In other stories, Gjallarhorn is given to Heimdallr, the god responsible for keeping watch over the realm of Asgard. Once Odin has drunk from the well, he becomes the wisest of all of the gods. Despite losing his eye, he is able to see more than any of them due to his immense knowledge.

In another one of Odin's myths, Kvasir, the eloquent god of poetry and wisdom (who had been formed from the spit of the Æsir and Vanir after the war), had taken to wandering and sharing his beautiful words and cleverness with all he met. When he comes across two particularly horrible dwarfs named Fjalar ("deceiver") and Galar ("shouter"), they kill Kvasir and drain all the blood from his body, then mix it with honey to make an enchanted mead they call Óðrœrir, the mead of poetry. They store the mead in three containers. When the gods search for Kvasir, the dwarves laugh together and say that he has choked on his own cleverness.

But worried the powerful gods will come after them, the dwarves persuade a giant, Gilling, to take them out to sea. Once they reach deep water, they overpower him, and he falls overboard. Unable to swim, he drowns. When the wicked dwarves return to the shore and tell her that Gilling has been killed in an accident, she cries out in grief. The dwarves dislike the sound of her wailing and kill her by dropping a millstone on her head.

These giants have a son named Suttungr ("heavy with drink"), who seizes the murderous pair when he learns what they have done to his parents. Pleading for their lives, they offer him their three containers of the mead of poetry they made from Kvasir's blood. Suttungr agrees. He hides it under the Hnitbjorg, a mountain, with his daughter Gunnlöd keeping guard.

Odin is determined to drink this mead and gain its powers, so he disguises himself as a farm laborer and goes to Suttungr's brother's farm, where nine men are working hard. Odin offers to sharpen their blunt scythes with a special whetstone. After he has attended to them, the scythes are razor sharp and quickly cut through the hay. The farmhands ask if they can buy the stone, and Odin agrees but cryptically warns them they will have to pay a high price. He throws it into the air. The men scramble for it, and in the tussle, they kill each other with their newly sharpened blades.

Odin then goes to the farm and tells Suttungr's brother that his men have killed each other in an argument. He says his name is Bölverkr ("worker of misfortune") and offers to do all of their work in exchange for a sip of Óðrœrir. The farmer replies that it is not his, but he agrees to speak to his brother.

After working on the farm as agreed, Odin and the farmer go to Suttungr, but the giant will not allow them anywhere near his mead. Odin has no intention of giving up. After making his companion drill through the rock of the mountain, he shapeshifts into a snake and slithers into the hole. He wriggles his way into the chamber where the lonely Gunnlöd is guarding the precious mead.

She initially refuses to give Odin any of it, but after he says he will sleep with her for three nights, she agrees to allow him a small drink from each of the containers. However, after the third night, the containers are empty since each of Odin's sips leaves them completely empty. Ever the charmer, Odin leaves, flying away in the form of an eagle.

Suttungr, realizing he has been robbed, comes lumbering after him. But as they approach Asgard, he is forced to give up his chase. The gods, having seen Odin as an eagle make his approach, set out containers. Odin regurgitates the mead he has swallowed into them. As he does this, some drips from his beak fall onto Midgard, and those who are touched by them become the poets and scholars of the human world.

As well as having an obsession with wisdom, Odin is just as fascinated by enchantments, spells, and less worldly knowledge. In the 10th-century Anglo-Saxon manuscript *Lacnunga*, Odin (as Woden) is mentioned twice in the Nine Herbs Charm, an ancient recipe for a magical spell used for healing and protection. In addition to his ability to shapeshift, he learns the Vanir witchcraft *seidhr* from Freyja and frequently consults völvas and soothsayers for advice.

In the final part of the *Völuspá* (itself translated as the "Witch's Prophecy" or "Sibyl's Prophecy ") from the *Poetic Edda*, an aged seeress reluctantly gives Odin the prophecy for Ragnarök, the end of the world, and the fate of all the deities in the Norse cosmos. Many of Odin's actions are often futile attempts to delay what he believes to be inevitable. His accumulation of the *einherjar* ("army of one," the souls of those killed in battle) at Valhalla, his diligent watchfulness over the nine realms, and his uncharacteristic benevolence and endless patience toward Loki (although they are bound as blood brothers) can all be seen as efforts to avoid the inescapable ending known as Ragnarök.

Chapter Seven – Valhalla and the Afterlife

As well as being the god of wisdom, healing, and poetry, Odin was, more importantly, the god of war and the dead or at least the god of slain great warriors. He welcomed the souls of Vikings who had been killed in battle—the most glorious dead—at his magnificent hall, Valhalla ("Hall of the Slain").

The souls of these most worthy warlords and celebrated soldiers were known as the *einherjar* ("army of one"), and they were destined to fight alongside the Æsir at the final battle of Ragnarök.

Several poems in the *Poetic Edda* (including *Völuspá* and *Grímnismál*) and the *Prose Edda* recount how the *einherjar* are selected from the dead on the battlefield by the Valkyries, an army of female warriors who are armed and wear helmets. They ride (or rather fly) on their horses over land and sea. In some stories, they are known as Swan Maidens because they disguise themselves as swans so they can fly away quickly.

In *Völundarkvida* in the *Poetic Edda*, three brothers who live at Úlfdalir ("wolf dales") notice three women spinning linen at the shore of a lake. When they see their swan garments nearby, the men realize the ladies must be Valkyries. They take them back to their homes, and the three couples live happily for seven years until the Valkyries fly off to battle, never to return.

In some myths, the Valkyries are said to be the daughters of Odin, but in the Eddas, they are more often princesses, the daughters of kings. In the poem *Helgakvida Hjörvardssonar*, a young prince sees nine Valkyries riding past him. One he describes as the "bright faced lady." She is Sváva, the daughter of King Eylimi, and she protects the young prince in many battles.

In the *Völuspá*, a seeress describes six Valkyries: Skuld ("fate"), who carries a shield; Skögul ("shaker"), Gunnr ("war"), Hilda ("battle"), Göndul ("wand-wielder"), and Geirskögul ("spear-bearer"). In *Grímnismál*, eleven more Valkyries are identified by name. It is explained that Skuld is also one of the Norns and has a special role as a Valkyrie since she "always rides to choose the slain and decide the outcome of battle."[6]

The Norse hero Helgi Hundingsbane's story is retold in two chapters of the *Poetic Edda*. Helgi was the son of Sigmundr and Borghildr of Brálund, whose story is included in the *Prose Edda*. On the night Helgi was born, the Norns determined his fate and decided he would be a great prince.

At the age of fifteen, Helgi disguises himself and infiltrates the court of the Saxon king Hunding, the enemy of his people, with an audacious plan to capture and kill him. Before long, the king grows suspicious of Helgi, and he is forced to make his escape in the dress of a bond-woman (a female servant) and hides away in a mill.

Soon afterward, Helgi takes an opportunity to kill King Hunding, which earns him his name, Helgi Hundingsbane. The king's sons demand that he pay them weregild, the blood fine levy due for murder, in lieu of revenge, but Helgi refuses. Instead, he leads his men into battle against these Saxon princes.

After the battle, in which he kills all of the dead king's sons, Helgi rests beneath Arastein ("Eagle Cliff") as Valkyries appear on the battlefield with "bolts of lightning; wearing helmets at Himingvani. Their byrnies [armor] were drenched with blood; and rays shone from their spears."[7] One of them, Sigrún, speaks with Helgi while still mounted on

[6] *The Poetic Edda.* Translated by Carolyne Larrington. Snorri Sturluson. Oxford University Press, 2014.

[7] *The Poetic Edda.* Translated by Carolyne Larrington. Snorri Sturluson. Oxford University Press, 2014.

her horse. She tells him how her father has betrothed her to a particularly despicable and ignoble prince, one of the sons of Granmar, king of the Hniflungs, whom she considers to be unworthy of her.

Helgi chivalrously gathers his men together, and they set sail for Frekastein to wage war on Granmar and his armies to save Sigrún from her forthcoming marriage. During the voyage, there is a great storm. Sigrún's intervention with Rán, the volatile sea goddess, saves all of their lives.

Upon their arrival at Frekastein, Helgi's men make their attack on Granmar's forces. As they fight, the Valkyries arrive to help them achieve victory. After it is over, the Valkyries fly away, leaving Helgi and Sigrún to marry.

They have several sons, but they do not live happily ever after. One of Granmar's sons, Dagr, survived, and he is bound by Viking honor to seek revenge on the man responsible for the slaughter of his father and his brothers. He prays to Odin, and after making the appropriate sacrifices and rituals, Odin gives Dagr his spear, which he uses to kill Helgi.

Dagr tries to give his condolences to Sigrún, but she is bereft and curses him, telling him he should spend the rest of his life in the forest eating only rotten meat for his cruelty. Then, she has a barrow prepared for her beloved. However, his soul is already in Valhalla, where he seems quite happy, especially since he has sufficient influence to have his old enemy, Hunding, made to feed the pigs and wash the *einherjars'* feet.

Meanwhile, Sigrún continues to pine for her husband. When a servant tells her she has seen him and his men riding into his funerary barrow, she runs to see for herself. There, she finds Helgi, but he is disheveled, his hair covered with frost, his hands wet, and his body spattered with blood. He tells her this is because her tears of grief continue to fall onto him. They spend the night together in his barrow, but the following day, Helgi returns to Valhalla, leaving Sigrún to mourn alone once more.

In Snorri Sturluson's *Heimskringla*, the best known of the old Norse king sagas, the earthly rituals necessary to prepare a warrior for Valhalla are described. The body was to be laid on a funeral pyre with all his possessions. Sometimes, even his wife and servants would be placed on the pyre so they would be there for him in Valhalla. Afterward, the ashes were to be spread on the ground or scattered on the sea.

Valhalla is described as magnificent and palatial. When the men are called to fight at Ragnarök, some 800 warriors will march out of its 540 doors. The *Poetic Edda* describes Valhalla as "rising peacefully" for the weary *einherjar* who approach its doors. In front of the main entrance stands a tree with red gold leaves called Glasir ("gleaming"), and the gates are guarded by wolves while eagles soar overhead. The hall has "spear-shafts for rafters, it's roofed with shields, mail-coats are strewn on the benches," and there are piles of the possessions that have been buried or cremated with the warriors for their long journey to the afterlife.

According to *Grímnismál*, Valhalla is located in Gladsheimr, and Thor's hall, Bilskirnir, is contained within its walls. In the *Poetic Edda*, an argument between Odin (in disguise as a ferryman) and Thor includes the revelation that the souls of dead thralls (the enslaved or serfs) reside in Thor's fields, Thrúdvangar.

Beyond Valhalla is the decidedly heavenly Gimlé, a world inhabited by angelic light elves. It is in Vidbláinn, a heavenly plain above Asgard. The brave souls that survive Ragnarök will be welcomed there.

Once the *einherjar* arrive at Valhalla, they can enjoy the Vikings' ideal life. There will be permanent and perpetual fighting and epic war games, often to the death. Before the great feast at the end of each day, all wounds are healed, and those who had been slain that day are reborn or at least breathe again.

It is not only the dead *einherjar* that are restored to life. Odin's unfortunate boar Særimner is slaughtered daily to feed this massive army, only to reappear and go through the same process the following day. He is butchered by Andhrímnir, the cook of the gods, then stewed to perfection in Eldhrímnir ("fire-sooty"), a great cauldron.

The feasting warriors also partake in copious quantities of mead that is provided by Odin's goat, Heidrún. She eats the leaves of the Læraðr tree at Valhalla and is milked for this magical mead by the busy Andhrímnir. The Valkyries then serve it. According to the *Prose Edda*, "there are still others whose duty it is to serve in Valhalla. They bring drink and see it to the table and the ale cups ... these women are called

Valkyries."[8]

In the *Prose Edda*'s *Skáldskaparmál*, Snorri presents a picture of a dining hall full of atmosphere. There is no lighting other than the gleaming swords of the *einherjar*. During the feasting, Odin does not eat any of the meat. He gives his share to his two wolves, Geri and Freki, his constant companions. He does, however, partake in Heidrún's excellent mead.

Although Valhalla is home to some of the fiercest and most brutal warriors, it would seem there are certain expectations in terms of etiquette. In *Skáldskaparmál*, the jötun Hrungnir ("brawler"), on his golden-maned horse Gullfaxi, is beaten in a race against Odin on his eight-legged horse, Sleipnir. When the race ends at Valhalla, Hrungnir is invited inside in the typical Viking spirit of extending hospitality. He quickly becomes inebriated and abusive, offending the assembled Æsir. When he brags that he will take Valhalla back to Jötunheim, they are heartily sick of his boorish company and summon Thor to deal with him. Drunk as he is, Hrungnir craftily reminds him that he is a guest of the Æsir and cannot be harmed. However, he is persuaded to leave Valhalla to indulge in a flyting (battle of words). In some versions of the story, Thor slays him with his hammer, Mjölnir, and takes possession of Hrungnir's wonderful horse.

The Wild Hunt, or Odensjakt ("Odin's ride"), in which Odin, on his horse Sleipnir, leads a great host of Valkyries, ghostly dead warriors, elves, wolves, and hawks in a thundering chase through the deep, dark forests, has been retold in northern European mythology, although there are some variations from region to region. Most Celtic and Germanic folklore describe the hunt as an omen of doom for those who are unfortunate enough to see it, but in Norse mythology, it is never seen, only heard. The ghostly sounds of a jostling crowd galloping at full pelt, hooves thundering, the clashing of armor and weapons, and Odin's hounds baying into the night would certainly be a haunting thing to hear.

Before the advent of Christianity, it was presumed these hunters were in pursuit of a boar or some mystical being that needed rescuing or destroying. Afterward, the hunters had a different quarry and were said to be running sinners to ground or hunting for children who had not

---

[8] *The Prose Edda—Tales from Norse Mythology.* Translated by Jesse Byock. Snorri Sturluson. Penguin Classics, 2005.

been baptized.

The remaining warriors who are not selected by the Valkyries for Valhalla go to Freyja's afterlife, Fólkvangr ("Field of the People"), a peaceful meadow where weary souls can take their rest. It is attested in both the *Prose Edda* and the *Poetic Edda* that Fólkvangr lies within Freyja's hall, Sessrúmnir.

In *Grímnismál*, Agnar learns from the disguised Odin that "Freyja decrees who shall have seats in the hall; The half dead each day does she choose, And half does Odin have."[9] Similarly, in the *Prose Edda*, "whenever she rides to battle she gets half her slain."[10]

The difference between the souls selected by the Valkyries for Valhalla and those taken to Freyja's Fólkvangr is not clear, but since the prophecy of Ragnarök calls for the *einherjar* to fight shoulder to shoulder with the gods, their existence at Valhalla can be regarded as a divine training program to prepare them for that time. Those enjoying Freyja's hospitality are, perhaps, the souls of the good and the honorable who lack the ferocity required for that last great battle.

In the old Icelandic *Egill's Saga*, which dates back to 1240 CE and tells the family story of the Viking Egill Skallagrímsson, a woman named Thorgerd says, "I have had no evening meal, nor will I do so until I join Freyja ... I do not want to live after my father and brother are dead." This would suggest that starving oneself to death was considered a sufficiently noble demise for the lower tier of dead heroes in the afterlife.

Freyja has another possible connection with the afterlife for the Norse people. The souls of unmarried women who die become attendants of Gefjon, according to the *Heimskringla* (one of the Old Norse kings' sagas, written by Snorri Sturluson). Although Gefjon is a goddess associated with agriculture in Danish myths, Gefjon was another name for Freyja by Norwegian Vikings. So, it is possible that, allowing for their names being muddled in the mists of time, it is Freyja who takes them. If that was the case, her halls host a rather more mixed crowd than Valhalla.

---

[9] *The Poetic Edda.* Translated by Carolyne Larrington. Snorri Sturluson. Oxford University Press, 2014.

[10] *The Prose Edda—Tales from Norse Mythology.* Translated by Jesse Byock. Snorri Sturluson. Penguin Classics, 2005.

For those who died at sea (surely an occupational hazard for the Viking raiders), there is no passage to Valhalla. The Norse sea god Ægir is widely accepted to be a jötun, albeit a particularly reasonable and friendly one. His wife, Rán, is sometimes described as his sister or a Vanir goddess, but the two have very different characters and purposes.

Ægir is associated with all the benefits of the sea, such as calm waters and fishing. He is also celebrated for his wisdom. Rán is the dangerous and cruel perpetrator of stormy seas and shipwrecks. She has a great net that she casts out into the depths to ensnare hapless sailors and then drags them down to her realm, where they will remain in her hall.

The Norse legends also suggest a possibility of reincarnation, especially through ancestry. In the *Saga of Hrómundar Gripsson*, Helgi Hundingsbane and his Valkyrie wife Sigrún were Helgi Hjörvardsson and his beloved Sváva in a previous life and Helgi Haddingjaskati and Kára in the next. There is also the suggestion that some of the dead did not leave their barrows or burial mounds but remained there, body and soul, to watch over their descendants and their homes. In the Icelandic *Eyrbyggja Saga*, there is a story about a shepherd who shares his vision of the mountain Helgafell opening up to receive a dead man (and worshiper of Thor). There, he finds his deceased family feasting and is happily reunited with his dead father.

Finally, there was Hel's realm. This was not quite the hell of Christianity. The *Prose Edda* suggests that all of the dead—other than those selected for Valhalla, Fólkvangr, or Rán's hall—enter Helheim. There are pleasant areas where flowers grow, and there is feasting. Baldr and Nanna are depicted in the seats of honor at one such occasion in *Gylfaginning*. Wicked people do not remain with Hel; they die again to plummet farther into the dreadful realms at the bowels of the Norse cosmos.

Chapter Eight – Freyja, the Goddess for All Seasons

Freyja ("lady") is often considered the archetypal Norse goddess. She is beautiful, ethereal, and strong. She and her brother (sometimes her twin) Freyr were born to Nerthus, the goddess of prosperity and peace. (It was believed that when she was among humans, no conflict or battle would occur.) Their father was Njörd, a major god of the Vanir who helped to oversee sailing, fishing, and prosperity.

Freyja was the goddess of love, fertility, magic, war, and death. She is sometimes referenced as a Valkyrie and even as their leader, being responsible for half of those who died in battle. These men were possibly deemed less heroic than those who headed to Valhalla because they do not appear to play a role in the final battle of Ragnarök and live a peaceful existence under Freyja's care.

There is scant information about Freyja prior to her move from Vanaheimr to Asgard. Since there are so many conflicting stories about her, it is likely that she has become confused with other goddesses, particularly Odin's wife, Frigg, whose name is not too dissimilar to Freyja. Even Freyja's husband's name, Ódr, can easily be muddled with Odin. It has been noted that the entity "Frija" could be a combination of Freyja and Frigg or even the two intertwining into one being. Gullveig, who was possibly the cause or a casualty of the Æsir-Vanir War, and Gefjon, the fertility goddess associated with plowing, have also been interwoven with Freyja throughout the years. The Christian monks who put the myths to parchment were likely not as concerned (or interested) in the goddesses. Since Freyja's name is synonymous with the word "lady," confusion was unfortunately inevitable.

The *Ynglinga Saga*, one of Snorri Sturluson's kings' sagas, presents Freyja as one of the Vanir's leaders in the Æsir-Vanir War. She worked closely with Odin to help oversee the peace settlement and took responsibility for the offering of sacrifices. In the same saga, Freyja is revealed as a völva, a seeress gifted in the mystical practice of *seidhr*, which she introduces to Asgard. (In the *Lokasenna*, she reveals that Frigg is also a gifted shaman who knows the fate of everything.) Freyja has also been seen as a destiny-weaving Norn, probably due to her gifts as a seeress, which is somehow fitting since her true–or original–story has been unraveled somewhere within the many strands of mythology, legend, and folklore.

Just as Odin has his spear and Thor his hammer, Freyja has a marvelous cloak made from falcon feathers that gives the wearer the ability to fly or shapeshift into a hawk. She travels in a chariot drawn by two black or grey Norwegian Forest cats or lynxes and is usually accompanied by her battle swine, Hildisvíni. In *Hyndluljód* of the *Poetic Edda*, one of Freyja's loyal followers (sometimes presented as her lover), Óttar, builds a shrine to her and prays for her to help him discover his ancestry after he has made a wager of everything he owns on the quality of his forefathers. Freyja appears to him and disguises him as Hildisvíni. The goddess rides on Óttar's back as they travel to see the jötun sorceress Hyndla. Freyja forces her to tell Óttar what he wants to know and also to give him a potion, *minnisöl* ("memory cup"), that will ensure all he has been told will not be forgotten. Since he is descended from several great heroes, he wins the bet and becomes a formidable Swedish king.

Despite being arguably the most popular of the Norse goddesses, Freyja exhibits some serious flaws. In *Lokasenna*, when Loki has his meltdown and accuses the Æsir of their many indiscretions and decidedly ungodly behavior, he airs some dirty laundry about Freyja. He states that she has slept with every god and elf present in the hall, which she denies. Freyja insists that he is simply trying to draw attention from his own misdeeds and bad behavior, then tells him to go home to lick his wounds. But Loki is by no means finished. "Be silent, Freyja! Thou foulest witch," he counters and crudely describes an occasion when the gods surprised her and her brother Freyr while they were enjoying sexual relations.

Freyja treasures her magnificent golden and amber necklace, the Brísingamen ("gleaming torc"). In the early 14th century story *Sörla páttr*, written by two Christian scholars keen to discredit the pagan gods and hoping to put an end to the customs being practiced in their names, Freyja is a mortal and one of Odin's favorite and avaricious mistresses. When she hears of a fabulous necklace (clearly Brísingamen, though this isn't stated) that has been created by skilled dwarf craftsmen, she cannot help but go and have a look for herself. When she sees it, she has to have it, whatever the price. The four dwarves agree to give it to her in exchange for her sleeping with each of them.

When Freyja refuses to tell Odin how she came by her fabulous jewel, Loki finds out and tells him. They decide to steal the necklace from her. Loki, a shapeshifter, turns himself into a flea and hops into Freyja's bed. When he finds her sleeping on her necklace, he bites her cheek, and she turns over. Loki then takes the necklace to Odin.

When Freyja realizes she has been robbed, she appeals to Odin. He tells her that he knows exactly how she had procured it and that he will only return it after she agrees to force two great kings to fight against each other in a perpetual war. Whenever one is killed, they will rise again to continue the battle. These bitter hostilities will continue until a Christian savior (namely Olaf Tryggvason, king of Norway from 995 to 1000 CE) will end this state of affairs.

There is certainly a missing myth about the theft of Brísingamen. In the *Prose Edda*, there is a story about how Heimdallr and Loki fight over the necklace while transformed into seals. Thereafter, Loki is referred to as the thief of Brísingamen. There are scenes of a battle between the two (though not as seals) carved onto the walls of an old mead hall and described in the poem *Húsdrápa*, written by the 10th-century historical poet Úlfr Uggason. Brísingamen also appears in the old English epic poem *Beowulf.*

This view of Freyja is countered by her devotion to her husband Óðr ("frenzy" or "inspiration"). The couple had a difficult relationship. Óðr, sometimes attributed as the god of sunshine and summer, is a curious character. He is restless and unsettled. He leaves Freyja for long periods, wandering and exploring foreign lands (like Odin) and enjoying the company of other women.

When he leaves the first time, Freyja is bereft. The land becomes cold and barren, plants and flowers wither, and nothing will grow. As she weeps, her tears fall on the earth and turn into gold. When she can no longer bear to be without him, she sets out to find him. Disguised, she travels from place to place, leaving gifts and blessings to everyone she meets along her way. She dares not reveal herself in case Ódr learns that she is near and flees until, eventually, she finds him one night sleeping underneath a tree. She quietly lays beside him. When he awakes, he is delighted to see her. He has grown tired of his travels but has been worried he would not be made welcome after his absence due to his womanizing. With the couple reunited, the bitter winter melts away, and the world grows more temperate. Flowers begin to bloom, and crops grow again.

In time, Ódr once more grows restless and feels compelled to leave. Again, the world is enveloped by winter snow. But Freyja knows he will be loyal to her and that he will come home. When he does, the warm summer sunshine will return as well.

Freyja and Ódr share two daughters, the beautiful Hnoss ("jewel") and Gersemi ("treasure"), who are possibly one and the same. In *Skáldskaparmál*, Hnoss is referred to as Freyja's "gold-wrapped glorious child" and Freyr's niece. In *Gylfaginning*, there appears to be only one daughter: "Hnoss is the name of their daughter. She is so beautiful that from her name whatever is beautiful and precious is called Hnossir."[11]

Freyja (and Frigg) have probably suffered more than most of the Norse deities during Christianization. Freyja's name, especially in the plants and places named after her, were often replaced with that of the Virgin Mary, perhaps inevitably since Freyja translates as "lady". The wildflower milkwort *Polygala vulgaris*, that was known as Freyja's hair in Scandinavia was later renamed after the Virgin Mary.

Though the confused and vague picture that remains gives Freyja an unworldly and ethereal quality that befits the held view of the Vanir, the Vikings saw her in a much different light. She was revered as a goddess of war and earthly love, and they believed rituals and sacrifices to her were a necessary part of life.

---

[11] *The Prose Edda—Tales from Norse Mythology*. Translated by Jesse Byock. Snorri Sturluson. Penguin Classics, 2005.

Chapter Nine – Thor, God of Thunder

Thor ("thunder"), the muscular and mighty bearded warrior, is synonymous with Viking culture. He holds a special place in the Norse myths as the fearless, hot-tempered, and headstrong warrior and served as an inspiration to the men of Scandinavia in the Viking Age.

As a god, he was known for his benevolence toward humankind. Despite his father Odin being the All-Father, Thor seemed to have been worshiped more than any other Norse god, particularly in Iceland. Representations of his hammer, Mjölnir, have been found carved onto a great number of runestones and Viking artifacts. Thor's role is "defender of Asgard and Midgard," according to *Skáldskaparmal* in the *Prose Edda*. In the myths, he regards the jötnar as his enemy despite his paternal grandmother being the jötun Bestla and having a relationship with another jötun, Járnsaxa, mother of his son Magni. Magni is the only god other than Thor able to lift Mjölnir.

In the Eddas, Thor is married to the earth goddess Sif, who is known for her amazing golden hair. Wherever she walks, crops grow behind her. In *Gylfaginning* of the *Prose Edda*, it is revealed that she also had a son from a previous relationship, the handsome and all-round good guy Ullr, who is also a mighty warrior. She and Thor share a daughter named Thrúd ("strength"), who is likely a Valkyrie as that name is listed among them. It is widely held that there are missing myths about Thrúd, not least since the jötun Hrungnir is referred to as the "thief of Thrúd," but no story remains to explain it in any of the sources.

For the Vikings, Thor was the embodiment of thunder. The rumbling and crashing sounds were his chariot charging across the sky, while bolts of lightning were said to be his flashing hammer as he flings it far away to bring down the jötnar. Thor wears great iron gauntlets called Járngreipr, which help him to manage the immense power of Mjölnir, and his belt, Megingjörd, doubles his already legendary strength.

Thor drives a chariot pulled by two goats named Tanngrisnir ("teeth grinder") and Tanngnjóstr ("thin teeth"). In the *Prose Edda*, it is revealed that these goats also sustain the great god since they can be slaughtered each day. Thor then eats their meat. Provided the bones are left intact, Thor can resurrect them the following day using mystical powers from his hammer, Mjölnir.

In one myth, Thor and Loki stay the night with some peasants and share the goat meat with them. A boy, Thjalfi, breaks one of the leg bones to enjoy the marrow inside. The next morning, when the goats are brought to life again, Thor is angry to find that one of them is lame. When he finds out why, he takes Thjalfi and his sister, Röskva, to serve him. (In some translations, they are referred to as Thor's slave children.)

Thor noticing the lame leg of one of his goats.
https://commons.wikimedia.org/wiki/File:Tanngrisnir_and_Tanngnj%C3%B3str_by_Fr%C3%B8lich.jpg

The four leave the peasant's small holding and venture into the forests of Jötunheim. By nightfall, cold and tired, they find a large empty building and sleep inside. The next morning, they discover that it is actually a glove of the jötun giant Skrymir, who does not see them. The following night, they sleep in a nearby clearing, but Skrymir is sleeping nearby under a massive oak tree. His snoring is so loud that the earth shakes.

Thor, thinking the sleeping giant is vulnerable, takes Mjölnir and strikes Skrymir's head three times with all of his might. This appears to have little effect, but Skrymir awakens and, after stretching and opening his sleepy eyes, notices Thor. The god of thunder quickly has to think on his feet and asks the giant his name.

Once they have made their introductions, Skrymir tells them that he thinks some acorns and bits of foliage must have fallen during the night as he felt something drop on his head. He also warns the group that if they are heading for Útgarda-Loki's castle, they should modify their boastful and arrogant attitude.

Thor, Loki, and the children soon find themselves outside Útgarda-Loki's castle, a structure so immense they have to crane their necks to see its full height. The gate is closed, and Thor cannot pry it open, so they are forced to ignobly squeeze through the bars. They then find themselves in a great hall with giants seated on two benches. The ruler of the castle, Útgarda-Loki himself, eyes the group beadily.

He tells them that in order to enjoy his hospitality, they each have to perform a feat, with the exception of Röskva. Loki quickly volunteers to demonstrate his famous talent for eating. He is given a huge platter of food and competes against a giant named Logi, who eats far more quickly than the god of mischief, leaving the trickster god defeated.

Thjalfi declares that he is a fast runner, so a race is arranged between him and a diminutive man named Hugi. They race three times, with Hugi decidedly beating Thjalfi every time.

Finally, it is Thor's turn. First, he tries a drinking contest. Despite taking three colossal drafts, he is soundly beaten. Then, in a trial of strength, he finds himself unable to lift a large grey cat, only managing to raise one of its paws with a great deal of effort. Thor loses his temper and demands that he should wrestle one of the giants in the hall. None of them will fight, saying Thor is clearly an unworthy adversary. Útgarda-Loki calls for his nurse, Elli, a wizened old woman, to fight, and she and

Thor begin to grapple. Again, Thor is hopelessly outclassed, and Elli brings him down. Afterward, Útgarda-Loki, as good as his word, gives them rooms for the night after they have eaten.

The next morning, the demoralized group is welcomed by their host, who asks them how they feel about the contests the night before. Thor tells him he cannot understand how he could have failed so badly and fears for his reputation. Útgarda-Loki reveals that he and Skrymir are one and the same and that all isn't as it seemed. The three blows that Thor had made to the giant's head while he was sleeping were so mighty that they had almost killed him and created great valleys in the landscape. In his contest, Loki had been pitted against a wildfire that quickly devoured all in its path. Thjalfi had raced against thought, and Thor had lowered the level of the sea with his drinking. The cat he had tried to lift was actually the serpent Jörmungandr. When he lifted its paw, he had actually held it up into the sky. The old woman Elli was, in fact, old age, something that no one can beat.

After telling them that they were actually formidable opponents, Útgarda-Loki says that he hopes they will not meet again. The furious Thor starts to swing his hammer, but the giant and the castle disappear.

In another myth, retold in both the *Poetic Edda* (*Hymiskvida*) and the *Prose Edda* (*Gylfaginning*), the sea god Ægir and his wife Rán plan a feast for the Æsir at their great hall underneath the waves. However, they need a cauldron big enough to prepare mead for all their invited guests. The god Tyr knows that the jötun Hymir has the largest, and Thor volunteers to go to Jötunheim in order to obtain this cauldron.

Hymir is not happy to see Thor since the god is a friend of Midgard. Nevertheless, he prepares for Thor's stay by slaughtering three bulls. By the first evening, Thor has already eaten two of them. The next day, Hymir, annoyed by his guest's ridiculous appetite, suggests a fishing trip and sends Thor to find some bait. Rather ungraciously, Thor returns with the head of the largest of Hymir's remaining bulls. Nevertheless, the two row out to sea. Hymir is delighted to catch two whales, but Thor seems nonplussed and starts to row the boat farther and farther out into deeper waters. Hymir protests, reminding Thor that it is the domain of the horrible serpent Jörmungandr, but Thor continues until he finally casts his line. Soon, it is clear that Thor has hooked the monster. Sea water begins to pour over them as it thrashes around on the end of Thor's line, and the boat threatens to fall apart.

Alarmed, Hymir shouts at Thor, telling him to let Jörmungandr go, but Thor, well aware his destiny is to fight it to the death, refuses and stands firm in the disintegrating boat. As the serpent's head emerges from the water, Thor takes his hammer to finish it off. Just as he is about to strike, the terrified Hymir cuts the line. Jörmungandr lives to fight another day. Thor is furious and, with a roar, throws Hymir overboard. He then returns to Asgard with the jötun's kettle and the two whales slung over his shoulder.

In the *Poetic Edda* (*Hymiskvida*), the story is similar, but at the point when Thor catches the serpent, volcanos erupt, and a great earthquake causes Thor to lose his grip. Jörmungandr slips back into the sea. Afterward, Hymir takes Thor back to his hall and challenges him to try and break his indestructible cup. Thor smashes it against his head and then quickly leaves with the cauldron while being pursued by giants.

In the prophecy of Ragnarök, Thor will battle Jörmungandr to the death, and in some ways, this myth whets the appetite for this great, final fight.

Before that terrible day, Thor has a particularly stressful adventure when his beloved hammer, Mjölnir, is stolen. Realizing it is missing, he calls upon Loki, telling him he suspects one of the jötnar has stolen it. Loki borrows Freyja's falcon feather cloak and flies over Jötunheim to the hall of Thrym.

The jötun readily admits stealing Mjölnir and tells Loki that the Æsir cannot hope to find it. He has buried it deep underground, but he will return it if Freyja becomes his wife.

Loki returns to find Thor waiting for him. When he learns of Thrym's demand, he tells Freyja that she should get ready for her wedding. Unsurprisingly, Freyja will have none of it and leaves the Æsir to sort out the dilemma themselves. Without Mjölnir, the citadel is far more vulnerable to attack from marauding jötnar.

Finally, Heimdallr suggests a crazy plan. Thor, whose stature is such that the rainbow bridge of Bifröst cannot support his weight, should dress as the lovely, willowy Freyja. With a veil, Thrym and the jötnar will be fooled. Thor is very reluctant to embrace his femininity, but he finally agrees when he realizes it is the only way he will be reunited with his hammer.

Dressed for marriage and wearing the precious necklace Brísingamen, Thor sets out with Loki beside him, who is dressed as his handmaiden.

When Thrym sees he will have his "bride," he prepares a magnificent wedding feast that befits the great goddess Freyja.

An early 20ᵗʰ-century depiction of Thor dressed as Freyja.

The wedding party prepares to feast, and the veiled bride drinks an ocean of mead and consumes an entire ox before her betrothed has even started eating. Then, "she" devours eight sizeable salmon, one after the other, without pause, before eyeing some of the other delicacies.

Before Thrym grows too suspicious of his bride's astonishing appetite, Loki tells him that Freyja was so excited at the prospect of marrying him that she had been unable to eat for more than a week. This assuages Thrym's doubts for a while. The quick-thinking Loki is also able to explain Freyja's beard and angry, growling voice.

Boldly, the jötun leans over and lifts his bride's veil a little, revealing Thor's eyes that burn like fire. Alarmed, he turns to Loki, who explains that Freyja has also been unable to sleep in anticipation. By then, most of the jötnar wedding guests are growing uneasy.

One of Thrym's sisters asks the bride for a bridal token to seal their friendship, but the veiled bride stays silent and does not move. Thrym, anxious to please Freyja, demands that Mjölnir should be brought to the table so she can see he is honorable.

As soon as the hammer is within reach of Thor, he throws off his veil and swings Mjölnir, calling upon all of his power and might. With great claps of thunder and flashing bolts of lightning, Thor fells several jötnar and destroys the hall, with the burning roof and walls collapsing to crush the remaining guests as he and Loki depart in a cloud of thunder.

Thor fighting against giants.
https://commons.wikimedia.org/wiki/File:M%C3%A5rten_Eskil_Winge_-_Tor%27s_Fight_with_the_Giants_-_Google_Art_Project.jpg

Chapter Ten – Legendary Creatures from Norse Myths

The Norse realms are inhabited by creatures and entities that are much harder to identify with than the gods but still provide wonder and fascination. Some creatures are "fairer to look on than the sun," such as the Ljósálfar (light elves) of Álfheim, while others inspire fear, revulsion, and horror.[12]

Only the barest of details are known about the light elves, who are ruled over by Freyr. Regularly in the company of the Vanir and the Æsir, they appear to be made welcome amongst the gods and goddesses. There are elves enjoying Ægir's feast and then looking on aghast, presumably, at Loki's vicious and foul-mouthed flyting in *Lokasenna* in the *Poetic Edda*. Some later stories based on the myths suggest that Freyr and Freyja are elves and that Vanaheimr and Álfheim have become one and the same.

There is also the suggestion that light elves are the equivalent of angels. In the *Prose Edda*, it is revealed that there are other realms beyond the nine, but they are so remote and abstract that they are barely known to the wisest beings of the (known) Norse cosmos. One is Andlàngr, which shelters the souls of the dead after Ragnarök and is "south of and above this heaven of ours." Above this realm is Gimlé,

---

[12] *The Prose Edda—Tales from Norse Mythology.* Translated by Jesse Byock. Snorri Sturluson. Penguin Classics, 2005.

and above that is Vidbláinn. The character High admits, "We believe it is only light-elves who inhabit these places for the time being."[13]

Volündr, the master smith married to the Valkyrie Hervör, is identified as an elf, but his actions are somewhat vengeful and grisly for such an ethereal and virtuous being even considering the provocations he endured. In the *Poetic Edda*, in *Völundarkvitha*, he is revealed to have been captured by King Nithuth, who cuts his hamstrings to prevent him from escaping before setting him to work on the island of Sævarstod, where he will make precious trinkets. The story then becomes increasingly dark. When the king's sons visit his workshop, the elf promptly kills them. "The evil was open when in they looked; He smote off their heads, and their feet he hid."[14] He then makes chalices from their skulls for their father, jewels from their eyes for their mother, and brooches from their teeth for the king's daughter. He then rapes the king's daughter and leaves her pregnant with a son, Vidga (a character in several Scandinavian ballads). Volündr flies to the royal palace on mechanical golden wings he has fashioned (in some of the myths, he uses the swan cloak of his Valkyrie wife) to tell miserable King Nithuth what he has been up to. This myth, which has several variations, is known as Wayland the Smith in Old English and also appears in Old German, Old Frisian, and Old French traditional folk tales.

The light elves' cousins, the Dökkálfar, are represented in several myths in the Eddas, as well as sagas and folklore. Many of them are mentioned by name.

Skáldskaparmál in the *Prose Edda* talks about how Mjölnir is created. The god of mischief, Loki, finds Thor's wife, Sif, sleeping and thinks it will be a great joke to cut and steal her wonderful golden hair. When Thor returns to find Sif weeping, her head shorn, he is incensed with anger. When he catches up with Loki, he grabs him by the throat and shakes him like a rat.

Begging for mercy, Loki says he will get the dwarves to make Sif a crown of beautiful hair. It will be even better than the locks he had taken from her. Against his better judgment, Thor makes Loki swear to it and

---

[13] *The Prose Edda—Tales from Norse Mythology.* Translated by Jesse Byock. Snorri Sturluson. Penguin Classics, 2005.

[14] *The Poetic Edda.* Translated by Carolyne Larrington. Snorri Sturluson. Oxford University Press, 2014.

releases him. Thor loves his wife and cannot bear to see her so distressed.

Loki goes to Svartálfheim and asks one of the dwarf craftsmen to make Sif a crown of golden hair that will magically attach itself to her head and grow like natural hair. He promises anything the dwarf asks in return.

The dwarf and his companions are delighted to have the opportunity to impress the gods. They state they will provide the lovely hair and two more gifts: a spear that will never miss its target and a ship that will always find a favorable breeze and can be folded up so that it can fit into its owner's pocket. Delighted, Loki takes these treasures to Asgard and insists that these dwarves cannot be matched for their craftsmanship to anyone who will listen.

A dwarf called Brokkr hears Loki's boasts and believes his brother, Sindre, can make even better items and tells him so. When he speaks up, Loki airily tells him that if he can make three better treasures, he can have his head!

Sindre begins to work on a pigskin that he throws in his furnace. Brokkr works the bellows to create the intense heat required for special enchantments. While he labors, a gadfly bites Brokkr's arm, but the dwarf resolutely continues to blow. Then, Sindre throws a golden ring on the fire. As Brokkr gets to work with the bellows again, the gadfly returns and bites his neck hard. Still, the dwarf takes no notice and continues his work.

Finally, Sindre puts an iron in the fire, and Brokkr determinedly takes up the bellows again. This time, the gadfly (which is often thought to be Loki in disguise) bites him between his eyes. This bite is so severe that Brokkr cannot see what he is doing. He stops working for a moment to brush the fly away.

Their work done, Brokkr takes their treasures to Asgard, where Thor, Odin, and Freyr have agreed to judge the contest. First, Loki gives Sif her crown of hair. She is delighted her beauty has returned. He then gives Odin the spear and Freyr the ship.

Brokkr gives Freyr a golden boar that is as fast as any horse. Its bristles shine so bright that they can make a dark night as light as day. He then gives Odin a gold armlet that will multiply into nine every ninth night. Each new armlet will be just as large and heavy as the first. Finally, he gives Thor the hammer Mjölnir and tells him it will never fail. No matter how far he throws the hammer, it will always return to him. Its only fault is the shortness of its handle, which had been caused by the momentary lapse while operating the bellows. Once Thor has tried the hammer, the gods agree that Brokkr and Sindre have won the contest.

Loki tries to escape, but Thor brings him back. Brokkr demands his prize: Loki's head. Eventually, Loki agrees that he will have to accede, but, with a flash of genius, he says he will not allow Brokkr to touch his neck (a story reminiscent of Shylock's bargain in Shakespeare's *The Merchant of Venice*). Brokkr was not altogether defeated. He took an awl and tightly sewed Loki's boastful lips together.

Brokkr and Sindre are much more reasonable and sympathetic characters than many of the dwarves in Norse mythology. Fáfnir was the son of Hreidmar, another dwarf, and had two brothers named Ótr and Regin. One day, Odin, Loki, and the god Hœnir were at the waterfall of Andvari, who was an incredibly wealthy dwarf who could turn himself into a pike at will.

When Loki spotted an otter, he killed it for its fur, not realizing it was the shapeshifting dwarf Ótr. As the gods continued, they came across Hreidmar's dwelling. They intended to sleep there, but as soon as their host saw Loki's otter pelt, he angrily demanded his son's blood- price (weregild).

Loki and Odin went back to the waterfall to find Andvari's treasure beneath the water. As they pulled up his mystical gold-finding ring and his Helm of Awe, Andvari watched, full of resentment, as he was powerless to stop the gods from taking his wealth. All he could do was curse the treasure, promising misfortune on anyone who possessed it.

The treasure is given to Hreidmar, and the gods continue on their way. However, Fáfnir is suddenly gripped by avarice. He kills his father, and to stop his surviving brother from getting his share, he takes Andvari's treasure into a forest cave and remains there, guarding it jealously.

As his hoard grows, thanks to the enchanted ring, Fáfnir's evilness catches up with him. He gradually transforms into a terrible dragon.

Regin, Hreidmar's remaining son, wants to avenge his father. He crafts a magical sword and gives it to Sigurd, the legendary Norse hero, who agrees to set out on a quest to slay the dragon.

Sigurd finds Fáfnir's cave and works out where he goes to take a drink. He digs a trench there, and the dragon soon falls into it. Sigurd slices its belly open with his sword. As he dies, Fáfnir warns Sigurd about the curse.

Regin asks Sigurd to remove the dragon's heart and roast it over a fire. As he attends to the flames, he burns a finger. When he puts the injured finger to his mouth, he ingests some of the dragon's blood. Immediately, he receives an incredible gift: he can understand the language of animals. As Sigurd listens to the birds chattering, he learns that the treacherous Regin is planning to kill him so he can take the treasure for himself. Sigurd takes his sword and kills Regin as he sleeps and then eats Fáfnir's heart and drinks the other dwarf's blood for good measure. Then, having accrued greater wisdom and understanding, he leaves with Andvari's treasure.

In the *Skáldskaparmál* of the *Prose Edda*, which Snorri Sturluson based on the 10th-century Slavic poem *Haustlöng*, Thor agrees to a duel with the stone-headed (and stone-hearted) jötun Hrungnir. The jötnar are aware of Thor's prowess in battle, so they are uneasy at the prospect of this fight. Hrungnir's defeat would mean dishonor for them.

The jötnar decide to dredge the river at Grjotunagarder. They used the clay from the riverbed to build a massive giant. This giant is so large that his head is partly obscured by the clouds. The jötnar give their creation a mare's heart, and when it slowly comes to life, they name it Mist Calf (or Mökkurkálfi).

Thor and his servant Thjalfi arrive for the fight. Thjalfi fools Hrungnir into thinking that Thor is coming at him from underground. Hrungnir, armed with a whetstone, is then surprised by Thor's hammer, Mjölnir, flying toward him. Quickly, he flings his stone, but as the weapons make contact in mid-air, the hammer smashes the stone into tiny fragments that fly in all directions. The pieces that fall on Midgard formed whetstone quarries.

Mjölnir continues flying toward Hrungnir and strikes his stone head, crushing it. As he falls down, dead, Thor is trapped underneath one of the giant's huge legs. While Thor is stuck, Thjalfi attacks the giant's legs with his ax until the clay giant topples over, shaking the ground as he falls.

Eventually, Thor's son, Magni, lifts Hrungnir's leg, freeing Thor. However, Thor is left with a fragment of the whetstone stuck deep in his head, which causes him a lot of pain from time to time.

Other mythological creatures that may have been well known to the Vikings include Selkolla, a lovely young woman with the head of a seal. However, the earliest known account of this strange being is in the *Gudmundar Saga*, which recounts the life of Bishop Gudmundur Aragon (1161–1237). That is more than a century after the Viking Age came to an end. Similarly, Fossegrimen, a kind of water spirit, and huldra, forest sirens that lure young men into peril with their lovely voices or harp music, are considered part of Norse folklore but are not thought to have been popular during the Viking Age.

Chapter Eleven – Loki, the Trickster God, and the Beginning of the End

The most complex and contradictory of the Norse gods–if he is, in fact, a god at all–is Loki. Unlike the other deities, he has no clear area of responsibility, and there is no known hall in which he resides in Asgard, Vanaheimr, or Jötunheim. He is a wanderer with no fixed abode.

Loki has no known cults or worshipers amongst Viking or early Norse cultures. There is a possibility that Loki evolved through the ages and is actually derived from two entities: the trickster Loki of the Eddas and a "domestic spirit," or *vættr,* who lived under the fireplace and helped with farm work to bring wealth to the farm. This is thought to be the root of Loki's long-held association with fire, something that is not alluded to in the Eddas at all.

To add to the confusion, the traditional Norwegian folktale character Askeladden, "Ash Lad," is closely associated with Loki. They certainly share a similar intelligence and courage, but Askeladden is generally a neglected boy, forced to sleep in the ashes of the fireplace but goes on to achieves greatness, wealth, and status (much in the vein of the rags-to-riches Cinderella story). It is difficult to see much of the modern vision of Loki in the story of Askeladden.

Loki plays a role in almost each of the Viking myths. He is frequently presented as the Æsirs' problem solver. He often—but not always—

arrives to alleviate situations that he has had a hand in. However, he is so much more than that. Loki is a shapeshifting clown, a trickster, a friend in need, a convenient scapegoat, and, as the stories draw to an end, a veritable demon. But prior to the Eddas, there is little evidence that Loki existed other than a few runestones that date from between 700 and 1000 CE that appear to depict scenes of myths in which Loki is a central character.

According to the *Gylfaginning* in the *Prose Edda*, Loki's father was the jötun Fárbauti ("cruel striker"), and his mother was the Æsir goddess Laufey ("leaves," or "foliage"), also known as Nál. He has two brothers, Byleistr and Helblindi. Other than their names, little is known of Loki's family.

From an early age, Loki aligned himself with his mother's race (this is made clear by his given name, Loki Laufeyson). In the *Lokasenna*, he reveals that he and Odin, who were both half jötun, at some time became blood brothers: "Remember, Odin, in olden days, that we both our blood have mixed." The two often travel together and seem to enjoy each other's company.

Although it is often argued that all of the Norse gods have flawed characters and indulge in decidedly unchivalrous and mean-spirited actions, Loki is something else. In the myths, he is portrayed as slippery, sly, scheming, cowardly, and reckless. Most of his schemes come to nothing, and he rarely ends with the upper hand for all his wily ways.

In a story that well illustrates his role in the myths, Loki, Odin, and Hœnir (one of the Æsir gods exchanged for Freyja, Freyr, and Njörd to settle the Æsir-Vanir War) are traveling in a remote, mountainous area. They are hungry and far from home when they come across a herd of oxen. The group decides to kill one of them to eat. But no matter how hard they try, the meat remains uncooked. The gods cannot understand how this can be until a large eagle perched in a nearby tree begins to speak to them. It reveals that it has enchanted the meat. If they promise to give him a share, he will release the ox from his spell. The gods agree, but once the dinner is ready, the eagle flies down and feasts on the best pieces of the meat. Annoyed, Loki takes a large stick and hits the eagle, but the giant bird clutches the stick in its talons and flies away with Loki still hanging onto it.

Loki shouts at the eagle, demanding to be set down. The great bird reveals himself to be Thjazi, the jötun sorcerer, and he makes Loki swear that he will bring him the goddess Idunn and her golden apples before setting him down.

After the three gods have returned to Asgard, Loki, mindful of the oath he had sworn to Thjazi, visits Idunn and tells her he discovered apples even more splendid than hers in a forest outside the fortified walls of Asgard. Curious, Idunn goes with him to compare them to hers, but Thjazi, in his eagle guise, is waiting and flies away with her.

Without Idunn and her marvelous fruit, the gods and goddesses soon begin to age. Greying, wrinkled, and increasingly infirm, they meet to find out where she has gone. Once they have ascertained that she was last seen leaving Asgard with Loki, they seize him and demand he should return her at once, or he will be killed.

Freyja lends him her magical hawk feather cloak, enabling him to shapeshift into a bird of prey. Loki flies off to Thrymheim ("thunder home"), Thjazi's great hall in Jötunheim. When Loki arrives, Idunn is all alone since her abductor is out fishing. Quickly, Loki turns her into a nut and carries her away as a hawk. However, Thjazi quickly gives chase when he returns to find Idunn missing. Loki arrives safely at Asgard and restores Idunn and her apples to the gods. He then organizes the building of a great fire in the realm's vast courtyard. Its flames set Thjazi's eagle feathers on fire. As Thjazi falls to the ground, the gods surround him, and he is killed.

Loki's antics often provide an element of comedy. Despite his propensity to trick and scheme, he is rarely the benefactor. For the most part, he is called on by the gods to right a wrong or alleviate a situation that is not necessarily of his own making.

In a vague passage in the *Poetic Edda*'s *Völuspá*, Loki's darker traits are explained by his eating some of a half-cooked heart (sometimes said to have been the Vanir goddess Gullveig at the time of her torture at the hands of the Æsir). This heart contained the soul of an "evil woman and resulted in him giving birth to three monsters: the goddess Hel, the wolf Fenrir, and the horrible serpent Jörmungandr. In other stories, these children were born from a relationship with the jötun Angrboda ("foreboding"), known as the "hag of the woods." Loki also had a family with his devoted wife Sigyn ("victory giver") and had one (or two) sons with her, Váli and/or Narfi.

In the myth of Baldr and Hodr, the sons of Odin and Frigg, we can see the evolution of the lord of mischief. He goes from a god who is always ready to help the gods when required with his tricksy, unconventional ideas and quick wits to a really unpleasant, sinister, and vicious character.

Baldr, the son of Odin and Frigg, was the god of light, joy, and summertime. He was loved by everyone, not just for his beauty and goodness but also for his wisdom, particularly for his talent for arbitration. He settled many arguments and disputes in Asgard and Midgard.

One night, Baldr and his mother dream the same vision that foretells his death. When Frigg tells Odin, he makes haste to Hel to find out if it is a prophecy. There, he finds a dead völva whom he resurrects. Although she is decidedly grumpy to be awoken from her final rest, Odin asks her to use her gifts to see into the future. She tells him that Baldr will die and that all of Asgard will mourn him.

When Odin tells Frigg what he has learned, she is determined that her glorious son will not die. She makes everything swear not to harm him; "fire and water ... likewise iron and metal of all kinds, stones, earth, trees, sicknesses, beasts, birds, venom, serpents."[15] Baldr was safe, or so everyone believed. Since they are so sure, it becomes a regular game to throw spears and weapons at him. They feel safe in the knowledge that he will be unharmed.

However, Loki feels irritated by Baldr's immunity to harm. He shapeshifts into an old woman and asks Frigg if it is true that she really convinced every single thing to take her oath. She concedes that she didn't bother with the humble mistletoe since it was so young.

The god of mischief scuttles off to find a sprig and makes it into a dart. When he finds the gods making their usual sport and Baldr enjoying the fun, he gives the mistletoe to Baldr's brother, the blind Hodr, and encourages him to join in. Loki even guides his arm so the dart finds its target. Hodr mortally wounds poor Baldr. As he lies dying, Odin whispers into his son's ear. These words, though important, have been lost, but the act itself is referred to in the Eddas (such as in *Gylfaginning* of the *Prose Edda*). It is generally presumed that Odin told Baldr that he would survive Ragnarök.

---

[15] *The Prose Edda—Tales from Norse Mythology.* Translated by Jesse Byock. Snorri Sturluson. Penguin Classics, 2005.

The death of Baldr.

Frigg, almost mad with grief, asks for someone to go and beg Hel to release her son. Hermod, Baldr's brother, takes Odin's horse, Sleipnir, to ride on for the long journey to Helheim. He finds Baldr there, lonely and miserable, and entreats Hel to release him as he had promised Frigg. He tells her that Baldr is the most beloved of all the gods and that everything is mourning for his loss. Hel agrees to release him on the condition that everything must weep for him first.

Everything does weep: gods, humans, animals, plants, and even stones cry out in grief. All that is except for an old giantess named Thökk, who is Loki in disguise. This giantess just sits in her cave and refuses to weep. Devastated, the Æsir are forced to accept that Baldr is lost to them. His body and Nanna, his wife, are placed on his ship, *Hringhorni*, which is then set ablaze at sea. This rite is commonly associated with the Viking tradition but likely didn't take place, at least not on the scale most people assume.

Odin wants to punish the killer of his dead son. He has two sons with the giantess Rindr. In a particularly unpleasant account in the *Gesta Danorum*, written by Saxo Grammaticus in the 13th century, Odin makes her mad and then rapes her. These sons, Vídar, the silent god of vengeance, and Váli, the god of revenge, reach maturity in a day. Váli kills his half-brother, the blind Hodr, just as he had been born to do.

According to *Lokasenna* ("The Flyting of Loki") in the *Poetic Edda*, Loki becomes infinitely more malevolent and unpleasant after Baldr's death. As the gods gather at the island of Hlesey in the hall of Ægir, the hospitable sea god, Loki takes one of his host's servants and kills him. Outraged, the gods throw Loki out. After licking his wounds in the forest, he barges back into the hall where the gods and goddesses have resumed their feasting.

The assembled gods are appalled, but Odin insists Loki should be allowed to sit. He warns the trickster god to behave. Loki is having none of it, though. He accuses the god Bragi of being a coward and his wife, Idunn, who is trying to prevent him from reacting, of being wanton and sleeping with her brother's murderer.

Loki then turns on Odin. He mocks Odin's interest in *seidhr* as being unmanly and compares him to a witch. Odin dryly points out that he is not the one who has born several children. Frigg tries to calm the situation by suggesting they should forget the past and move on. Loki has other ideas and accuses her of being a whore and sleeping with Odin's brothers while Odin was away.

Eventually, Loki makes the fatal mistake of revealing that he was behind Baldr's death. Freyja, furious, tells him that Frigg already knows that even if she has not said it, whereupon Loki accuses her of sleeping with every god and elf in the hall. When she tells him he is lying and warns him that he will regret his words, he accuses her of sleeping with her brother.

Njörd, Freyja's father, does not improve matters. After suggesting that it does not really matter who sleeps with whom, married or not, he trades insults with Loki. The god of mischief makes further claims about incestuous relationships between the Vanir deities, which are not denied. At this point, the god Tyr points out that the Vanir god Freyr is "the noblest of all the brave gods," but Loki rounds on him and reminds him that he lost his hand to Fenrir, Loki's son.

Freyr speaks up for Tyr and is insulted. Next, Loki tears into Freyr's servant, then Heimdallr, and then Skadi, who tells him, "You won't be at large, twirling your tail, much longer. The gods will bind you to a boulder with the guts ripped out of your ice-cold son." Loki fires back that he led the party that captured and killed her father, the jötun Thjazi.

Sif, Thor's wife, attempts to calm the situation, protesting that she is "wholly guiltless," but Loki counters that he has enjoyed a night with her. Turning to Freyr's other servants, he makes some particularly vile and xenophobic remarks as Thor enters, raging, having heard some of what Loki has had to say.

Thor threatens Loki, who, in turn, calls him "the son of the earth," Loki reminds him of some of his more embarrassing escapades (namely his failures in the jötun Útgarda-Loki's hall) and mockingly reminds him of the prophecy and the end of the Æsir. Loki finishes by ominously telling the gods and goddesses that this will be their last feast and then walks out, leaving them (presumably) shaken and appalled.

Loki is well aware that he has gone too far, but there is no going back, not least because he has publicly revealed that he was responsible for Baldr's death. He flees to a remote area in the far reaches of Asgard, where he builds himself a hidden cabin with several doors from which he can watch and easily escape if his enemies approach.

Paranoid, anxious, and worried the Æsir will catch up with him, Loki often leaves his home in the form of a salmon. He leaps into the boiling waters at Franang's Falls, but he still does not feel safe and returns to his cabin.

The next day, as Loki sits by his fire, fretting and wondering what to do, he anxiously knots together some lengths of twine and soon arranges them in such a way that he finds he has inadvertently constructed a fine net.

At the same time, Odin has found Loki from his throne, Hlidskjalf, high above Asgard. A group of gods sets out to capture him. As they draw near, Loki hears them. He throws his net into the fire and runs for Franang's Falls, where he becomes a salmon once more.

The party of gods enters Loki's cabin and finds it empty. But when they notice the ashes from the net Loki had made and realize it is some device for catching fish, they sit in the cabin, painstakingly recreating it. Once it is complete, they take it to the falls where Loki, as a salmon, is hiding. Thor casts the net into the water. Loki manages to avoid capture during the first two attempts, but on the third, he is caught in the net. He tries to jump away, but Thor grabs him and holds him tight. There is no escape this time.

Some of the gods take Loki to a dark cave, while the others go after Loki's sons, Váli and Narfi. They turn Váli into a wolf, and he immediately turns on his brother and tears him apart before turning tail and bounding away in the direction of Jötunheim. The gods remove poor Narfi's entrails and take them to the cave where Loki is lying, no longer a fish. He refuses to look at any of them or even speak. Then, the gods take their revenge. They tie him to a great slab of stone with Narfi's entrails that become as hard as iron once he has been restrained. Loki's wife, Skadi, brings a horrible snake, which is fastened over him in such a way that its poison will drip onto his face.

And there Loki remains, just as Skadi said, bound and helpless in a dark, damp cave. However, Loki is not alone. Skadi chooses to remain with him, devotedly holding a wooden dish above his head to catch the dripping snake venom. When it is full, and she leaves to empty it, the snake's poison that drops onto Loki's face makes him struggle so much that it causes the earth to tremble.

THE PUNISHMENT OF LOKI.

The punishment of Loki.

https://commons.wikimedia.org/wiki/File:Louis_Huard_-_The_Punishment_of_Loki.jpg

79

Chapter Twelve – Ragnarök, Twilight of the Gods

"The sun turns black, earth sinks in the sea,
The hot stars down, from heaven are whirled;
Fierce grows the stream, and the life-feeding flame
Till fire leaps high, about heaven itself."

Völuspá, the *Poetic Edda*[16]

The end of the world, Ragnarök, is foretold in the Eddas. Uncharacteristically, the *Poetic Edda* and the *Prose Edda* are, more or less, in accord regarding the details of this Viking Armageddon.

It begins with the most bitter winters: three consecutive years of biting winds, ice, and snow. Nothing can grow, there is no food to be found, and civilized beings revert to savagery to survive. Fathers kill their sons, brothers slaughter brothers, and civilized society will be forgotten in a bizarre orgy of incest. "An axe age, a sword age, a wind age, a wolf age," the völva summarizes for Odin in *Völuspá* as she describes the prelude to the great battle.[17]

---

[16] *The Poetic Edda*. Translated by Carolyne Larrington. Snorri Sturluson. Oxford University Press, 2014.

[17] *The Poetic Edda*. Translated by Carolyne Larrington. Snorri Sturluson. Oxford University Press, 2014.

The advent of the battle itself is heralded by Sköll and Hati, huge, hungry sky wolves who have been hunting the sun and the moon since their creation. They finally manage to catch and devour their prey with all the bloodshed and gore expected of such a demise. The skies are left dark and empty.

In this ominous prelude to the end, the Norns are fully occupied, busily weaving the strands of fate and deciding the destinies of the gods, jötnar, and humankind.

The world tree Yggdrasil starts to tremble, which causes the chains that hold the fearsome wolf Fenrir, who is in a state of frenzied rage after having been tricked and held captive for so long, to bend and break. Loki's other monstrous offspring, the colossal serpent Jörmungandr, rises from the sea. His frenzied writhing causes the horrible, ghostly ship *Naglfar* (made from the fingernails and toenails of dead men and women) to break its moorings and set sail for Vígrídr ("plain where the battle surges"), where the final conflict, according to the prophecy, will take place. *Naglfar*, which is sometimes said to be captained by Loki, carries the ice giant Hrym and his people. The ship will serve as a ferry to carry the frost giants to war.

Odin will understand that the day of Ragnarök has arrived after consulting the severed head of Mímir. He will then open the gates of Valhalla, and his army, the *einherjar*, armed and prepared, will march on Vígrídr. It is a field "a hundred leagues long and just as wide," according to *Vafþrúðnir* in the *Poetic Edda*. Odin leads them, along with the gods of the Æsir and Vanir.

At the same time, the sky will splinter and crack, allowing the fire giant Surtr-holding aloft his sword that gleams brighter than the sun-to lead the demons or fire giants from Muspelheim. They will storm over the rainbow bridge Bifröst, which crumbles away as they pass, alerting Heimdallr, the watchman of the gods. Heimdallr will blow Gjallarhorn, the enchanted horn that could be heard throughout all of the realms, calling everyone to war.

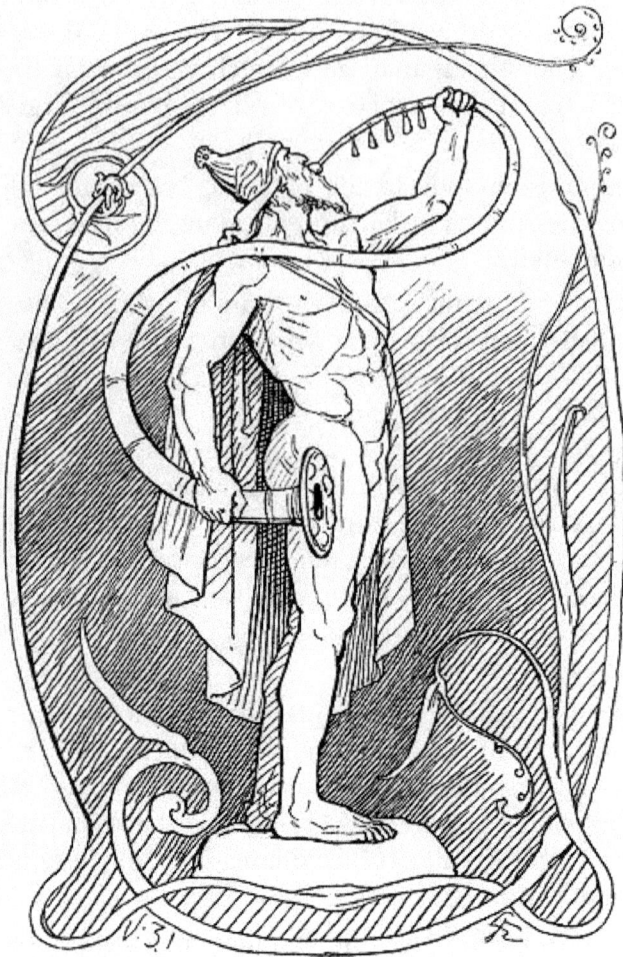

A 19ᵗʰ-century depiction of Heimdallr blowing Gjallarhorn.
https://commons.wikimedia.org/wiki/File:Heimdallr_by_Froelich.jpg

As Mímir's head falls to the ground, the *Völuspá* refers to Yggdrasil for the last time:

> "Yggdrasil shivers,
> the ash, as it stands.
> The old tree groans,
> and the giant slips free."[18]

---

[18] *The Poetic Edda.* Translated by Carolyne Larrington. Snorri Sturluson. Oxford University Press, 2014.

The final battle begins. The *einherjar* fight valiantly, just as they had practiced during their long stay at Valhalla. Fenrir approaches Odin, fire blazing from his eyes and nostrils. After a mighty battle, Fenrir devours his enemy. Odin's son, Vídar, the silent god of vengeance, exacts the revenge he was born for. He wears a shoe made from all of the leather ever discarded by the cobblers of Midgard. According to the *Gylfaginning* in the *Prose Edda*, he stamps on Fenrir's lower jaw and then grabs his upper jaw with one hand. With his other hand, Vídar drives his sword deep into the beast's throat, killing him.

Thor takes on his old enemy, the serpent Jörmungandr. After a grueling fight, Thor staggers back, victorious, but after taking nine steps, he, too, is dead, having ingested too much venom.

White and shining Heimdallr battles Loki, who has escaped his bonds. They kill one another. The powerful god of war, Tyr, wrestles the hellhound Garmr. (In the *Poetic Edda* poem *Völuspá*, his howls from Hel warn of the coming of Ragnarök.) They are both killed.

The Vanir god Freyr faces Surtr, but since he no longer has a weapon, having given his sword away during his courtship of Gerd, it is hopeless. Tyr is quickly slain.

With all the old gods defeated, Surtr raises his sword, and the realms sink beneath the sea, leaving a great void of nothingness. It is the end.

Time passes. Sól (or Alfrödull) had a daughter immediately before she was devoured by Sköll. The new Sól (as she was named) is just as beautiful as her mother and takes the reins of the chariot her mother once guided through the skies.

A new world begins to evolve. On the field of Iðavöllr ("splendor plain"), where the city of Asgard had previously been, the surviving gods assemble. Odin's sons Baldr and Hodr appear, as do their half-brothers Vídar and Váli, the latter having survived Ragnarök. Thor's sons, Magni and Mödi, are also there with Thor's hammer, Mjölnir. Presumably, there are also other goddesses and gods who survive, but they are not named in the Eddas.

These new gods set about creating a new world for themselves. "Shrines and temples they timbered high; Forges they set, and they smithies ore, tongs they wrought and tools they fashioned."[19] They build

---

[19] *The Poetic Edda.* Translated by Carolyne Larrington. Snorri Sturluson. Oxford University Press, 2014.

the shining city of Gimlé and live in a hall with a gleaming, golden roof.

As for humankind, a man named Líf ("life") and a woman named Lífprasir ("life of the body") manage to survive. They had concealed themselves in a wood (or tree) called Hoddmímis holt. As the worlds are reborn, they are sustained by the morning dew and worship Baldr. Because of them and their children, the world will be repopulated again.

"Now do I see, the earth anew

Rise all green, from the waves again;

The cataracts fall, and the eagle flies,

And fish he catches, beneath the cliffs."

Völuspá, the *Poetic Edda*[20]

[20] *The Poetic Edda.* Translated by Carolyne Larrington. Snorri Sturluson. Oxford University Press, 2014.

Conclusion

Few cultures continue to fascinate us like the Vikings, and the popularity of the Norse myths continues to endure.

The larger-than-life characters, their relatable qualities, and the fantastical worlds in which they exist have an irresistible appeal that has captured the imagination of writers, artists, composers, and performers through the centuries.

Shakespeare was influenced by Norse mythology. The witches in *Macbeth* could easily be Norns, and some of the relationships, particularly those between Loki and the other gods, are echoed in his plays. *Hamlet*, arguably Shakespeare's most powerful work, deals with revenge and moral corruption and is based on the ancient story of Amleth, the story of the Viking King Rorik's grandson. In the legend, jealous Feng slays his brother to marry Gerutha (Amleth's mother), and Amleth pretends to be mad to save himself from Feng's malicious intent. Feng sends his witless stepson to England with two of his men and a letter ordering his execution, but Amleth alters it so that it is an order for his escorts to be killed and for himself to be married to the king's daughter. Afterward, he returns to Jutland, where he finds Feng feasting with his nobles. Amleth burns the great hall and slays Feng to avenge his father. As the Eddas were not translated during his lifetime, Shakespeare became familiar with the stories from oral traditions or from long-lost accounts or plays.

The 19th-century composer Richard Wagner immersed himself in the *Poetic Edda* and *Prose Edda*, believing medieval culture held profound truths that might help explain the meaning of life. His operas, such as *Das Rheingold*, which tells the story of Andvari, the dwarf who forged a magic ring that was stolen by Odin (Wotan) to pay for the building of Valhalla, reflect his fascination with the subject.

J. R. R. Tolkien's *Lord of the Rings* is steeped in reimagined Viking mythology. For example, there is the use of runes and the various lands that compare to the realms of Midgard, Álfheim, and Svartálfheim. Tolkien interwove his lands and their inhabitants with real places and people. His central character, Gandalf, is often compared to Odin.

The mysterious, illusive, all-knowing, and bearded character with a whiff of sorcery, the All-Father, Odin, is a mainstay of fantasy and science fiction. This character offers protection and guidance to the good. His reflection can be seen in the *Star Wars* movies as Obi-Wan Kenobi and in the *Harry Potter* franchise as Professor Dumbledore. Dumbledore, just like Odin, has the thorny problems of prophecy to deal with.

In children's literature, the *Chronicles of Narnia* have more than a sprinkling of Christianized Viking mythology (Aslan's ancestor was Balder the Beautiful). The charming, award-winning animated show and books of the friendly Viking Noggin the Nog delighted and informed little ones in the last century. Players of the role-playing game *Dungeons & Dragons* are likely all too familiar with the various creatures and entities the Vikings revered.

More recently, Thor and Loki have captured the hearts and minds of a whole new audience with the Marvel comics, games, and blockbuster movies dedicated to the adventures of Thor and Loki. These battle-hardened warriors would surely appeal to the Scandinavian cultures from where they originated.

But for the Vikings and their forefathers, when life was hard and bewildering, stories of the nine realms, the gods, goddesses, and other beings, and the creation of the cosmos and its ultimate destruction helped them make sense of the world around them. The cycle of life and the inevitability of death, upon which the myths are framed, were concepts they were well used to. However, with the myths, they were better able to accept the chaos and unexplained.

The myths are so much more than interesting stories. They were cautionary tales that warned about the consequences of bad behavior, and they gave impressionable young Norsemen and women aspirational heroes. They provided gruesome horror stories to thrill and frighten, comedies to amuse and delight, and romances with beautiful characters overcoming the odds for their happy endings.

There cannot be many who have read or listened to Viking myths and legends without imagining old and wizened Norse elders huddled around a warm fire in the dark midwinter months with their extended families and telling the stories that they had learned as children with great relish and drama. Imagine the wide eyes of little ones, delighting in the adventures of Odin, the Æsir, and the Vanir, jeering as murderous dwarves get their comeuppance, and clinging to their mothers at the mention of Jörmungandr and Fenrir.

Through these extraordinary and complex stories, we can connect with the past and our ancestors. Although the Vikings are in the past, we can still celebrate this gift that will continue to endure.

If you enjoyed this book, a review on Amazon would be greatly appreciated because it would mean a lot to hear from you.

To leave a review:
1. Open your camera app.
2. Point your mobile device at the QR code.
3. The review page will appear in your web browser.

Thanks for your support!

Here's another book by Enthralling History that you might like

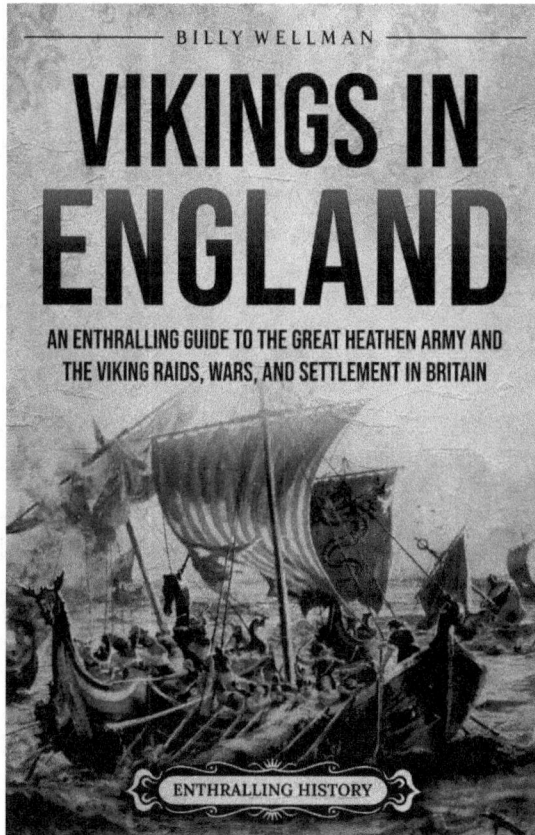

BILLY WELLMAN

VIKINGS IN ENGLAND

AN ENTHRALLING GUIDE TO THE GREAT HEATHEN ARMY AND THE VIKING RAIDS, WARS, AND SETTLEMENT IN BRITAIN

ENTHRALLING HISTORY

Free limited time bonus

We forget 90% of everything that we've read in 7 days...

Get the free printable pdf summary of the book you've read AND much, much more... shhhh...

Enter Your Most Frequently Used Email to Get Started

DOWNLOAD FREE PDF SUMMARY

© Enthralling History

Stop for a moment. We have a free bonus set up for you. The problem is this: we forget 90% of everything that we read after 7 days. Crazy fact, right? Here's the solution: we've created a printable, 1-page pdf summary for this book that you're reading now. All you have to do to get your free pdf summary is to go to the following website: **https://livetolearn.lpages.co/enthrallinghistory/**

Or, Scan the QR code!

Once you do, it will be intuitive. Enjoy, and thank you!

Bibliography

The Book of Viking Myths: From the Voyages of Leif Erickson to the Deeds of Odin, the Storied History and Folklore of the Vikings
Peter Archer (Adams Media, 2017)

The Vikings
René Chartrand (Osprey, 2016)

The Penguin Book of Norse Myths: Gods of the Vikings
Kevin Crossley-Holland (Penguin, 1996)

In the Days of Giants: The Book of Norse Myths—The Beginning
Abbie Farwell Brown (e-artnow, 2019)

Norse Mythology
Neil Gaiman (Bloomsbury, 2017)

The History of the Danes
Saxo Grammaticus (Translated by Peter Fisher and edited by Hilda Ellis Davidson, 1979)

Myths of the Norse Men from the Eddas and Sagas
H A Guerber (Obscure Press, 2010)

Mythology: Timeless Tales of Gods and Heroes
Edith Hamilton (Little, Brown and Company, 1942)

Norse Mythology: A Guide to Gods, Heroes, Rituals, and Beliefs
John Lindow (Oxford University Press, 2002)

Norse Mythology: Tales of the Gods, Sagas and Heroes
Mary Litchfield (Arcturus, 2018)

Teutonic Myth and Legend—An Introduction to the Eddas and Sagas, Beowulf, the Nibelungenlied, etc

Donald MacKenzie (Obscure Press, 2010)

The Elder Edda: A Book of Viking Lore

Andy Orchard (Penguin Classics, 2011)

Tales of the Norse Gods and Heroes

Barbara Leonie Picard (Oxford University Press, 1970)

The Children of Ash and Elm: A History of the Vikings

Neil Price (Penguin, 2022)

The Poetic Edda (Translated by Carolyne Larrington)

Snorri Sturluson (Oxford University Press, 2014)

The Prose Edda—Tales from Norse Mythology (Translated by Jesse Byock)

Snorri Sturluson (Penguin Classics, 2005)

Volume 2 of Symeonis monachi Opera omnia

Symeon of Durham. Edited by Thomas Arnold (Oxford University Press, 1965)